'Then'

In November 1994 the school ~~~~~~~~~~~~~~~~ ary since it was established at the previous Church ~~~~~~~~~~~ in 1844. The school and its children published a commemorative ~~~~ etter and produced a T-towel to help mark the occasion.

'Now'

On Tuesday 13th June 2017 the school celebrated its 50th Anniversary since its move to Heath Drive on the Kingshill estate. To mark the occasion, the school and its children published, using 'Kindle Direct Publishing' a commemorative book, this book. Its aim to help capture the history of the school as far back as 1822 and for our children to reflect on how things have changed since their school opened in 1967.

Contents

- St Mary's at 50! A letter of introduction.
- The History of Our School
- Historical Archives
- A celebration…
- Memories:
    - Spot the difference?
    - Staffing.
    - Communication.
    - School Reports.
    - Prayers.
    - Fashion from the 1960s and 70s!
- Year 3: 'Letters and e-mails'.
    - 3B; Mrs Bunce's Class photographs and articles.
    - 3M; Mr Martin's Class photographs and articles.
- Year 4: 'School life in 1967 and today'.
    - 4C; Mr Cox's Class photographs and comparative reports.
    - 4T; Mr Carr's Class photographs and comparative reports.
- Year 5: 'Popular culture of the 1960s.'
    - 5C; Miss Charlwood's Class photographs and historical reports.
    - 5R; Mrs Reynold's Class photographs and historical reports.
- Year 6: 'Was life better in the 1960s or today?'
    - 6G; Miss Gilliver's Class photographs and balanced arguments.
    - 6T; Mrs Thorne's Class photographs and balanced arguments.
- Acknowledgements

Headteacher
Mr A Cosslett BEd (Hons) NPQH

St. Mary's Junior School — WARE

Telephone: 01920 463641
Fax: 01920 484897

Heath Drive, Ware, Herts SG12 0RL
E-mail: admin@stmarys306.herts.sch.uk   School website: www.stmarys306.herts.sch.uk

'Enjoying our learning together'

13 June 2017

Dear all,

Re: St Mary's at 50!

St Mary's Voluntary Controlled Church of England Junior School in Ware was opened by The Right Reverend E M Gresford Jones DD The Lord Bishop of St Albans on 13th June 1967. Now 50 years later we celebrate its anniversary by publishing this book which reflects on how times have changed between 'Then & Now'!

We wanted to mark this event by not only making it fun, but as a learning opportunity too. The children have collaborated well in writing letters, e-mails, reports and arguments comparing school life and popular culture of the different times. They have used a variety of sources to gather their information including interviewing some of the school's first pupils and former teachers, photographs, books and the internet including archived video footage. The children came in non-uniform on Tuesday 13 June 2017 dressed in outfits from the late '60s and early '70s. I am happy to report that none of the children received the cane or slipper for poor behaviour, wrote lines that 'I must not…', had a blackboard rubber or piece of chalk hurled at them for not paying attention, or had to stand in the corner with the 'dunces' hat on! The children at the end of the week did take part in a 1960s/70s disco dressed accordingly and gazed in shock and disbelief at some of the adults and their dance moves!

We were visited by the Bishop of Hertford, Rt Reverend Dr Michael Beasley who led an assembly sharing a bible story about 'Celebration' and asked our children to reflect on its meaning through 'I wonder…' comments. Bishop Michael was then given a school tour by some of our pupil school councillors.

In this book we hope that we have captured through the images and writings the spirit of St Mary's as a school that has served its community well over the decades. A school that actually first opened as 'The Ware National Schools' on its original site in Church Street nearly 200 years ago in 1820.

Yours sincerely

Mr Andy Cosslett (Headteacher)

The History of Our School

St Mary's School, originally known as the 'Ware National Schools' came into being in 1820 in a small building in Church Street (formerly Dead Lane) which is the site of the Christadelphian's meeting hall. The vicar of St Mary's took up the challenge of raising the educational standards. In 1844, the schools moved along Church Street to new premises behind the church next to the Manor House. The head teacher lived in the house adjacent to the school.

A weekly charge of one penny was made for children attending the school. In addition, the children were required to attend Sunday school in line with the school's aim of 'making them good members of society'.

Alongside financial pressures were concerns about the children and their teachers. Early reports state that the children were often absenting themselves with excuses about 'nursing the baby' or 'going on errands'. Concern too about the teachers was raised after an inspection in 1846 reported that discipline was unsatisfactory, none of the children were clean and instruction was scanty. Even the master and mistress were labelled as of no great capacity and unfit for the job!

By the 1860s the Ware National Schools had become known as St Mary's National Infants, St Mary's National Girls and St Mary's National Boys schools to distinguish them from a second set of National Schools, known as the Christ Church schools, that were. erected on New Street.

The 1870 Forster's Education act allowed the state to set up its own schools. Following this, a new building in the Gothic style was opened in 1874 after a public subscription raised more than £600.00. These original buildings can still be seen on Church Street close to the church buildings.

At some time, probably after the Second World War, the school became a Voluntary Controlled School. On 13 June 1967 the new school opened as a Voluntary Controlled Church of England JMI *(Junior Mixed Infants)* School to help serve the new Kingshill estate. The church owns the land that the school buildings stand on and provide 3 governors to sit on its board, including the vicar of St Mary's. Initially the infant children moved to the new building with the Junior children remaining at the Church Street building until Kingshill Infant School opened in 1971 on the same site.

> *'The new building was not immediately popular with staff or children. To the staff it seemed noisy and was often too hot in summer or too cold in winter. There were also great distances to be covered to get to any part of the school. The children missed their "nooks and crannies" outside the old building and did not feel at home in the large open spaces of the new school grounds. Needless to say we soon all settled down in our new surroundings and appreciated its benefits' (Jean Hobbs 1997 p2)*

There is evidence of discussions between the Diocese of St Albans and the Local Education

Authority of Hertfordshire about whether, or not, Kingshill should also be a church school. The decision was not. St Mary's has been a church junior school ever since.

Today, the children of St Mary's come mostly from Kingshill Infant School, with a few entrants from other schools. When they leave us the majority go on to a Secondary School in Ware or Hertford, with the majority going to Chauncy School.

It is very pleasing that our school has moved on somewhat from its first inspection in 1846 and that we no longer have unsatisfactory discipline or 'scanty' teaching, let alone 'unfit' leaders! Our last inspection in 2014 stated that we are a good school, friendly and welcoming where pupils say they like their teachers and enjoy lessons. The school is managed well and runs smoothly day-to-day, with school leaders recognised for regularly checking the quality of teaching and learning to make sure pupils make good progress. What a difference 197 let alone 50 years can make!

The references below were used to support this article and it is with great thanks to Rev' Hugh Wilcock and Jean Hobbs for all their work in helping to capture our history.

- A letter from **Rev Hugh Wilcock** *(Vicar of St Mary's)* to **Mrs Liz Neville** *(Former Headteacher of St Mary's)* outlining the early history of the school: 26 July 1989.*
- Rev Hugh Wilcock's notes on education relating to his research on 'Ware in the early 19th Century' that accompanied the letter above.*
- A letter from Rev Hugh Wilcock to **Mrs Hilary Cliff** *(Former Acting Head of St Mary's)* referencing an 'ancient letter from 1969': 30 July 1997.*
- A letter from the Assistant Education Officer to **Rev Canon Crofts** *(St Albans Diocesan Office)*: 22 April 1969.*
- The 'Preface' taken from 'The Log Books of Ware St Mary's Schools: Selected by **Jean M.F.Hobbs** *(Deputy Head at St Mary's in 1967)*' first published by The Ware Society in 1997.*

* **'Historical Archives'** shown on the following pages will give you some further insights into our school's history.

It is with many thanks to the **Rt Reverend Hugh Wilcock** *(former Vicar of St Mary's Church and St Mary's School Governor)* for all his early research that has supported some of the information in this book.

Historical Archives:

- A letter from Rev Hugh Wilcock (Vicar of St Mary's) to Mrs Liz Neville (Former Headteacher of St Mary's) outlining the early history of the school: 26 July 1989.

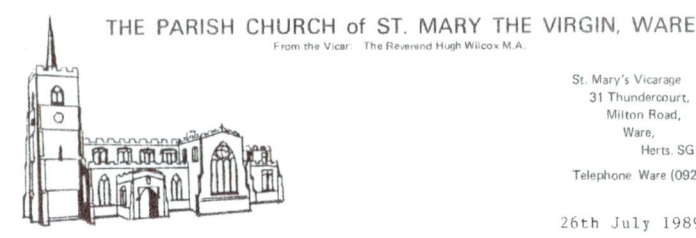

THE PARISH CHURCH of ST. MARY THE VIRGIN, WARE

From the Vicar: The Reverend Hugh Wilcox M.A.

St. Mary's Vicarage
31 Thundercourt,
Milton Road,
Ware,
Herts. SG12 OPT
Telephone Ware (0920) 46 4817

26th July 1989

Dear Mrs Neville,

re: The history of St. Mary's School

I noticed that in the papers circulated to potential applicants for staff vacancies at St. Mary's, there was a phrase which indicated a lack of precise information about the origins of the school.

In the course of my researches into the stormy 1840s in Ware I have been able to discover a little more, which I thought I should set down so that it is not lost sight of.

Attached are extracts from my draft notes, and you will see that in 1812 there was a "Sunday School" - an all day school teaching reading and writing, which suggests no day school had yet been founded, or if in existence, was not being used by many of the children. The "National School" was founded in 1820 in Dead Lane (now Church Street) on charity land which had formerly held the "Corpus Christi Barn" - the area now occupied by the Christadelphian's meeting room. By 1834 it had 95 boys and 72 girls as pupils.

It was to replace this school that the new St. Mary's School was built on the site behind the Church, the stone-laying ceremony being held on 23 May 1844.

The deed of conveyance (Chancery Close Role 1844 p.99 no.13) described the purpose of the new building as a "School for poor persons, and for the residence of a Schoolmaster and Schoolmistress, always in union with the National Society for promoting the Education of the poor in the principles of the established Church; to be under the management of the Vicar and jointly with the Curate or Senior Curate and William Parker Esq. (of Ware Park), Christopher Puller Esq. (of Youngsbury), and John Sworder of Ware, Maltfactor (and Churchwarden)".

From all this evidence I think it would be historically accurate to describe our present school as "the successor to the St. Mary's School built in 1844 on the Church Street site behind the Church, itself the successor to the first "National School" built further along Church Street in 1820".

With all good wishes,

Yours sincerely,

Hugh

(Hugh Wilcox)

Mrs Liz Neville
St. Mary's JM School
Heath Drive
Ware
Herts.

c.c. Mr. John Wood, Divisional Education Officer, Scotts House, Hagsdell Rd, Hertford

- Rev Hugh Wilcock's notes on education relating to his research on 'Ware in the early 19th Century' that accompanied the letter above.

Education

One of the contentious issues of the time was that of schooling; some of the most intransigent of landowners seeing education not only as an interference in the availability of labour, but also as a breeding ground for ideas which would encourgae folk to "get above their station". There was controversy too over the control of schools. Sunday schools, which in our time mean church organised activities for children on religious themes, began as an attempt to provide on Sundays, not only religious teaching, but basic instruction in reading and writing. The Gerish collection contains the 1812 rules for Ware's Sunday school. Children were to assemble at 8.30 am, were to go to Church morning and afternoon, and school ended at 6.00 pm. They were taught alphabet, spelling, reading, and to repeat the Lord's Prayer, the Creed and the Catechism. "Children not coming to school in time are to wear a Mark inscibed Idle Boy or Girl in large letters during church, and the whole or part of the School time; children behaving ill to wear a Mark of Naughty Boy or Girl." A Sunday school of this kind was the precursor of the day schools which were soon to be founded. The National Society had been founded in 1811.

Whereas Pigot's 1826 Directory lists three Boarding Acadamies, at Thunderhall, (gentlemen), Baldock Street and Back Street, (ladies), the 1833 edition shows much more diversity. There is the Charity school for girls in Church lane taught by Mary Gull; Susan Cobham (was this John's wife?) runs a school at Baldock Street, as does Ann Crabbe at Bluecoat Yard. The Revd Salisbury Dunn is in charge of a boarding school in Amwell End. The curate, The Revd James Britton is master of the Free Grammar School, in the building which stood where the Telephone Exchange now stands, beside the churchurchyard. Joseph Dives was master of the Lancastrian school (an independent nonconformist foundation) in Dead Lane, close to the National School (under the auspices of the National Society sponsored by the Church of England) whose master was William Miller. The Misses Teed had taken over Thunder Hall as a boarding school.

We know from a return completed by the Vicar of Ware in 1834 that the Lancastrian School had 109 pupils; that the National schools had 95 boys and 72 girls, the charity school for Boys, by which he presumably meant the Free Grammar School, had 10 pupils, and that there was a small school in the workhouse.

- A letter from Rev Hugh Wilcock to Mrs Hilary Cliff (Former Acting Head of St Mary's) referencing an 'ancient letter from 1969': 30 July 1997.

THE CHURCH OF ENGLAND   DIOCESE OF ST.ALBANS
THE PARISH CHURCH OF ST.MARY THE VIRGIN, WARE
HIGH STREET, WARE. (01920 462539)

	The Vicar:	
Assistant Priest:	The Reverend Canon Hugh Wilcox M.A.	Lay Minister:
The Reverend Margaret Beazley	St.Mary's Vicarage	Mr Geoffrey Voss
38 Fanshawe Crescent	31 Thundercourt	21 Queen's Road
Ware	Milton Road	Hertford
Herts SG12 0AS	Ware, Herts SG12 0PT	Herts SG13 8AZ
(01920) 462349	(01920) 414817	(01992) 554676

30 July 1997

Dear Hilary,

The enclosed photo-copy of an ancient letter from 1969 raises some interesting questions which may help in our discussions with the legal departments of the local authority and the Diocese regarding the site, legal ownership and so on.

You will see from this letter that it is quite clear that the Junior School was built first on the site and this suggests that the entire site was seen as the successor to the old St Mary's buildings in Church Street.

This piece of history indicates how close we came to having the Infant School as a Controlled School as well; such a pity that this did not happen.

With good wishes,

Yours sincerely,

(Hugh Wilcox)

Mrs Hilary Cliff
Acting Head
St Mary's J M School
Heath Drive
Ware
Herts

Enc.

cc. Mrs Liz Neville

Parish Administrator: Mrs Debbie Cock (01920) 462539
Director of Music: Mr Michael Smith GRSM, ARCO, ARCM
(01920) 821281

- A letter from the Assistant Education Officer to Rev Canon Crofts (St Albans Diocesan Office): 22 April 1969.

Dear Canon Crofts,

We have included in the 1969/70 [...] a project to [...] Infants school at Kings Hill, Ware. This is in fact very closely tied up with the Church of England controlled schools in Ware. The St. Mary's schools in the centre of Ware occupied old and unsatisfactory buildings. In the later 1940's a new Infant school was built on a site in Park Road. In recent years the Junior school has been built on a 2 form entry site at Kings Hill. Both are controlled schools. The Junior school is however operated in conjunction with the old St. Mary's buildings in the centre of the town as a J.M.I. school and the school at Park Road is also in process of becoming a J.M.I. school. The process will be completed in September. The question now arises as to the status of the new infant school which will go on to the Kings Hill site. Our feeling has long been I think that the new infant school should be controlled and that at the same time the primary school at Park Road, which is known as St. Catherine's should revert from controlled status to County status.

On Friday last Miss Bedington and I met Mr. Whitley the Vicar of St. Mary's and Chairman of Governors of both the St. Mary's school and the St. Catherine's school. He is anxious that the St. Catherine's school should remain controlled and he would like, in addition, the new infant school to be controlled, though if this could not be so he would prefer the infant school to be County rather than that St. Catherine's should lose its controlled status.

The controlled status springs of course from the old St. Mary's schools. As the infants school was provided at Park Road it attracted controlled status and the Junior school at Kings Hill similarly. Now that an Infant school is to be built at Kings Hill it ought to take St. Catherine's controlled status. Overall in Ware there would then be 2 form entry accommodation in county primary schools, approximately 1½ in the Church of England Aided school at Christ Church, 2 form entry controlled accommodation at Kings Hill and St. Catherine's would give the third 1 form entry county school. This we feel would give a better balance.

I have set this out at some length because it is fairly complex. Now that the job is in a building programme we should like to get the question of status resolved and I wonder if we could have a word about it fairly soon.

Yours sincerely,

Assistant Education Officer.

ST. ALBANS DIOCESAN OFFICE
24 APR 1969
RECEIVED

The Rev. Canon C.A.Crofts

- The 'Preface' taken from 'The Log Books of Ware St Mary's Schools: Selected by Jean M.F.Hobbs' first published by The Ware Society in 1997.

PREFACE

It was in September 1963 that I started teaching at Ware St Mary's JM School. My early teaching experience had been in Tottenham in a large JM School and afterwards I had done some home teaching in London and in Southampton.

In 1963 the school was in the old buildings in Church Street behind St Mary's Church. Besides using the school rooms and the hall within the two-storey building, we also used the Vicar's Room which fronts Church Street and the Scout Hut at the back. The classes at that time were of forty children or more and the children were placed in A, B or C streams. My memories of those times include the chestnut trees which overhung the boys' playground and were of special interest in the Autumn; the skill of the games of football played in the very confined space with the fear of balls going over into the Manor House garden; school dinners which were provided in the Congregational Hall and involved a walk through the back streets there and back supervised by members of staff; and of staff climbing out of a window half-way down the stone staircase to sit on the flat roof overlooking the boys' playground on sunny days in the summer, this providing a good vantage point to observe the behaviour below.

The Old St. Mary's School, Church Street, Ware

During the following twenty five years that I spent at the school many changes took place. The most fundamental was the building of the new school on the Kingshill estate. As Ware was rapidly developing the decision had been made to change the former Park Road Infants' School into a JMI School. This school had previously supplied the majority of our children, the remainder coming from Musley Infants' School. This in turn meant that St Mary's had to have its own infant school to serve the new Kingshill estate. Initially the older pupils remained in the old school building whilst the younger children and the new

THE LOG BOOKS OF WARE ST MARY'S

infant classes started in the brand new building until Kingshill Infant School was built next door and the juniors could all be together again. The new building was not immediately popular either with staff or children. To the staff it seemed noisy and was often too hot in summer and too cold in winter. There were also greater distances to be covered to get to any part of the school. The children missed their "nooks and crannies" outside the old building and did not feel at home in the large open spaces in the new school grounds. Needless to say we soon all settled down in our new surroundings and appreciated its benefits.

The idea to collect information from the school log books came about by my making use of the earliest one as source material for the children when we were studying the Victorian period. This book along with census returns of 1871 for Church Street and Crib Street gave us fascinating insights into life at that time around the school. Also, we started a newsletter for parents and we sometimes included excerpts from the log books recorded 100 years before. I realised that all kinds of information could be gleaned from the log books which were acting as contemporaneous history books of the period when they were written. Besides the general interest that local people might have in the school, a collection like this could be used as easily accessible material for children and students.

It has taken me a long time as initially almost everything was noted down by hand on cards using different sections. Eventually a computer was acquired and a great deal of selection was done whilst still retaining the original section arrangement.

My thanks are due to many people who have helped me in this enterprise. Jane Shropshire did the initial proof reading and raised helpful questions. The managers and Head Teacher of the present St Mary's school trusted me with the Log Books and the Head Teacher of St Catherine's School lent me their precious first Log Book. The staff at the Record Office and the Local Studies Library were always helpful - Eileen Wallace and Dr Kate Thompson in particular gave up some of their valuable time to assist. The Ware Society and the Ware Museum Society are giving some funding which is much appreciated. The Ware Society have agreed to publish this work under their name so that it will reach a larger audience. John Watkins of Herts Display has given useful technical advice but the two people who have helped me the most have been my younger daughter, Lindsay Mitchell, and David Perman. Lindsay has done all the tidying up of the text, etc despite her very busy, stressful life. David Perman has assisted me greatly and the introduction setting the St Mary's Schools in context of the history of education in Ware in largely his work.

A celebration...

Memories

We were visited by some of the school's earliest pupils who joined in our celebration assembly, bravely volunteered to be interviewed by some of our current children to help with their research before going on a school tour to bring back some fond memories. With many thanks to (from left to right); Mark, Melanie, Jill, Roy and Kevin.

'I remember getting into trouble for banging on the library carpet and covering the books in dust. As a punishment I had to clean all the books and wipe off all the dust. We had a very strict music teacher, we didn't mess around with her. She didn't have a class but took us for music lessons and played the piano in assembly.' **Mark Berry 1973 to 1977**

'I remember when the swimming pool opened – no heating, walking from changing rooms in the main school building to the pool with a towel round me. The water was not heated! Summer fairs every year were a highlight including a fancy dress parade.'
Melanie Ray 1969 to 1976

'Top junior class used to have "jobs", boys took it in turns to change the hymn sheets for assembly by climbing up the wooden climbing frames in the hall during assembly. Girls took it in turns for two of them to go to Kingshill shops to do the teachers shopping (including cigarettes!)' **Jill Homer 1969 to 1976**

'I played football for the school and you used to have to get changed in the classroom. There were large hymn sheets on a big book which used to hang from the ceiling in the hall. Teachers I remember were Mrs Sharman, Mrs Hobbs, Mrs Shropshire, Miss Burton, Mr Tanner, Mrs Crane, Miss Cox, Headmaster was Mr Winter.' **Roy Hall 1967 to 1974**

'How nice to return to St Mary's after all these years. The memories came flooding back. Mr Crown, Mrs Hobbs, Mrs Shropshire, Miss Burton. All the above teachers gave us a wonderful education and start in life. I used to love playing outside in the school grounds, singing in the choir and school sports days. I played football for school and enjoyed all my years here.' **Kevin Speller 1967 to 1972**

...being interviewed by our children

It was also great to welcome back Mrs Margaret Meldrum, a former St Mary's teacher and long serving governor to the school. Margaret brought in some pictures of our classrooms over the 1980's and 1990's to share with the children.

Kevin's cap…

Mr Kevin Speller kindly brought in his old school cap. We had never realised that the boys in the early days were expected to wear caps to school. It was also interesting that the school colours of 'burgundy' haven't changed that much over the years.

….not quite the fit that it once used to be!

Spot the difference?

Mrs Margaret Meldrum, one of our former teachers brought in a number of photographic prints from the 1980s and 1990s. We have tried to match each photograph, but can you spot the difference between **'THEN'** and **'NOW'**?

1983: Year 6 Christmas play in the hall.

2017: School hall from a similar angle.

1989: Year 4 classroom.

2017: Year 4 classroom

1990: Year 5 classroom

2017: now a Year 3 classroom

1996: Music and movement in the hall with a Year 4 class.

2017: Dance in the hall with a Year 6 class.

1996: Year 4 newspaper tower challenge.

2017: Year 4 a Mr Cox challenge!

...**how many differences did you spot?**

Staffing.

Then;
Headmaster: Mr Winter.
Teachers: Mrs Hobbs (Deputy Headteacher), Mrs Sharman, Mrs Shropshire, Miss Burton, Mr Tanner, Mr Crown, Mrs Crane, Mrs Kilford and Miss Cox.
School Secretary: Mrs Cox. **Caretaker:** Mr Wilson. **Welfare Officer:** Mrs Barnaby

Now;
Headteacher: Mr Andy Cosslett.
Teaching Team:
Mr James Martin (3M), Mrs Joanna Bunce (3B), Mr Peter Cox (4C), Tom Carr (4T), Mrs Fiona Reynolds (5R), Kerry Charlwood (5C), Miss Sarah Gilliver (6G and Deputy Headteacher), Mrs Clare Thorne (6T and Assistant Headteacher), Mrs Laura Taylor and Miss Louise Corbett (Class teachers), Miss Alison George (Inclusion Leader, R.E. and Collective Worship Leader, and Environmental Studies Specialist Teacher), Mrs Emma Norris (Cover Teacher), Miss Rebecca Bullar (PE Specialist Teacher), Mrs Collette Quinn (Violin Teacher).
Teaching Assistant Team:
Mrs Karen Tutin, Mrs Kerry Munt, Miss Charlotte Stagg, Mrs Claire Shropshire, Mr David Faint, Mrs Kathy Peters, Miss Rebecca Bullar.
Administration and Premises Team:
Mrs Joanne Scripps (Business Manager), Mrs Judy Wareham (School Secretary), Ms Tracey Powell (Resources Manager), Mr Graeme Wrenn (Site Manager), Mr Peter Boyle (ICT Technician)
Midday Supervisory Assistant (MSA) Team:
Miss Charlotte Stagg, Miss Rebecca Bullar, Mrs Claire Shropshire, Mrs Marie Grigg, Mrs Lynne Bassom, Mrs Katie Dare, Mrs Frances Tunks, Mrs Emma Baker, Mrs Natalie Hornsey, Mrs Mungai Balagopi
Catering Team (Caterlink):
Miss Kathryn Byron (Cook Manager), Mrs Paula Steele (General assistant)
Clerk to the Governors:
Mrs Jan Duff
Chair of Governors:
Mrs Nicci Smith

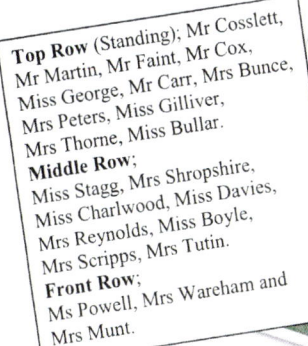

Top Row (Standing); Mr Cosslett, Mr Martin, Mr Faint, Mr Cox, Miss George, Mr Carr, Mrs Bunce, Mrs Peters, Miss Gilliver, Mrs Thorne, Miss Bullar.
Middle Row;
Miss Stagg, Mrs Shropshire, Miss Charlwood, Miss Davies, Mrs Reynolds, Miss Boyle, Mrs Scripps, Mrs Tutin.
Front Row;
Ms Powell, Mrs Wareham and Mrs Munt.

Communication.

Then;

Newsletters

150th Anniversary Edition
From Old to New

November 1994

Welcome to our newsletter to celebrate the **150th anniversary** of the founding of our school. We will be writing about the history of the school and all the exciting activities we do today. We hope you enjoy reading it and that you will treasure your memories of the school in the future.

New School opened

St.Mary's School, originally known as the National school came in to being in 1844. The original buildings, much added to, can be seen in Church Street next to the Manor House and close to the church building. The vicar of St Mary's took up the challenge of raising the educational standards.

A weekly charge of one penny was made for children attending the school. In addition the children were required to attend Sunday school in line with the school's stated aims of "making them good members of society".

Alongside financial pressures were concerns about the children and their teachers.

Early reports state that the children were often absenting themselves with excuses about 'nursing the baby' or 'going on errands'. Concern too about the teachers was raised after an inspection in 1846 reported that discipline was unsatisfactory, none

Stamp Collectors

The introduction of the Penny post 4 years ago (1840) by Rowland Hill has been hailed as a great success. Previously, the cost of a letter was calculated on distance and the money was collected on delivery. Hill's proposition of a flat charge for letters regardless of distance has been welcomed by all.

of the children were clean and instruction was scanty.
Even the master and mistress were labelled as of no great capacity and unfit for the job!

Education reforms

The 1870 Education act allowed the state to set up its own schools. Following this, a new site was found for the school and it then opened in 1874. These original buildings can still be seen in Church Street close to the church building. The head teacher lived in the house adjacent to the school. Some time after the Second World War the school became Voluntary Controlled.

Modern building

In 1966 the new school opened on the present site, infants also attending until the construction of Kingshill in 1971. During this time the old school was used as an annexe.

By the Children of
Mr Horner's class.

Now;

School Website

School Reports.

Then;

Hertfordshire County Council

WARE ST. MARY'S J.M. SCHOOL

Kingshill School,
Heath Drive,
Ware.
Tel: Ware 3641

REPORT FOR YEAR 1970 – 71

Name: Kevin Speller   Age: 10yrs 1mth   Class: 2C

	Effort.	Attainment.	Remarks.
ENGLISH Reading	2	C	Maintaining his position.
Creative Writing	2	D	More sustained concentration needed.
Comprehension	2	C	
Handwriting	2	C	
MATHEMATICS	2	C-	Fair grasp of basic number processes. Disappointing test result.
SPECIAL APTITUDES Art, Craft, Music, P.E. etc.			
SOCIAL ATTITUDE			Pleasant, friendly disposition.

General Progress: Kevin is a steady plodder, and has made progress over the year commensurate with his innate ability.

G. R. Crown.
Class Teacher.

Gradings:
EFFORT:- 1. Above Average 2. Average 3. Below Average.
ATTAINMENT:- A – Exceptionally Good
　　　　　　　B – Good
　　　　　　　C – Average
　　　　　　　D – Below Average
　　　　　　　E – Very Poor
Plus and Minus signs may be used.

J. K. Elswick.
Acting Headmaster.

HERTFORDSHIRE COUNTY COUNCIL

ST. MARY'S J. M. SCHOOL, WARE

REPORT FOR THE YEAR 1976/7

Name: Mark Berry   Age: 11.3   Class: 4S

Mark's behaviour and attitude to his work and play gave us cause for concern at the beginning of the year. In the last term however he has become far more settled and subsequently the standard of his work has improved considerably.

He reads and comprehends very well. His stories are adequate but he could give them more thought.

He has a good understanding of mathematical processes and copes well with new work.

Mark enjoys art, craft and games.

He is a boy who tries hard to please — he needs plenty of praise and quickly becomes despondent when things do not go well for him.

ENGLISH   B-   READING   B   MATHEMATICS   B

Gradings: A - Exceptionally Good.
           B - Good.
           C - Average.   I wish Mark success   J. Chapman
           D - Below Average.   at his new School   Class Teacher
           E - Very Poor.

Plus and Minus signs may be used.

                                                          Headmaster

Now;

End of year report: Fredricca Bloggs

Class Teacher Overview

Fred is a polite, funny and reliable member of the class who I have enjoyed teaching this year. Fred consistently tries her best and is always enthusiastic about learning in all areas of the curriculum. She is equally adept at learning independently and collaboratively, whether this is in pairs or small groups. Academically, Fred has continued to make good progress this but it is her social development, widening her group of friends, and growth in confidence, in sharing and volunteering ideas and thoughts, which I have been most impressed with. Fred is not deterred by setbacks and learns lessons from her mistakes during class, especially in mathematics when she embraces these to progress her learning. Fred has displayed a creative side during this year and I hope she continues her enthusiastic approach creative tasks so this potentially can be recognised. I have enjoyed teaching Fred, not least due to her fantastic sense of humour, and I wish her all the best for Year 5 and beyond.

Effort and Attainment

Subject	Effort	Below	Within	Upper within	Above
Reading	S		●		
Writing	E			●	
Mathematics	E				●
Science	G			●	

Key:
● Current attainment   E: Excellent   G: Good
                        S: Satisfactory   NI: Needs improvement

Reading

Fred has a fantastic approach to reading and is working above age related expectations for someone her age. She seems to really enjoy reading and often takes a book outside Reader programme we use at school and has not only year, but often surpassed it. This is a fantastic ach and 11 months, which is brilliant for her age. One ar support her answer, when answering questions. Alth be when reading aloud and I feel the more opportun open to discussing books she does and does not enjo

Target: To use the text to justify inferences drawn

Writing

Fred has continued to make great progress with her Fred consistently tries her best during her writing c year, She has a great attitude towards the writing p Fred normally writes good first drafts but it is her to publish some fantastic pieces of writing, notably has improved her handwriting during Year 4 but is s uses a great vocabulary for a person her age. Fred l writing.

Target: understand which letters, when adjacent to

Mathematics

Fred has continued to develop her mathematical und currently working just above age related expectatio notably geometry and statistics and has mastered s understanding of the multiplication and division fact She should however continue to practise over the ho working out has improved as the year has progresse uses formal written methods well for all four operat or the inverse operation to check her answer looks r

Target: To use estimation before answering a calculation check answers.

Science

Fred can ask relevant questions and use different types of scientific enquiry to answer them. She can set up practical experiments ensuring a fair test is carried out. Fred can record findings using scientific vocabulary, drawings, bar charts and tables. She can use scientific evidence to answer questions or to support her findings. She can identify that animals, including humans, need the right types and amount of nutrition and that humans and some other animals have skeletons and muscles for support, protection and movement. She can compare and group together a variety of everyday materials on the basis of whether they are magnetic or not. Fred can explain how and predict whether magnets attract or repel each other. She can recognise that she needs light in order to see things and that light can be reflected from different surfaces. Fred can explain the part that flowers play in the lifecycle of flowering plants including seed dispersal. She can describe how fossils are formed and recognise that soils are made from rocks.

Physical Education

Fred has a great attitude towards all PE lessons. She has particularly enjoyed basketball and sportshall athletics this year. She understands the importance of warming up and cooling down and has confidence when performing. She has developed some skills and tactics in a many different areas of games. Fred can describe effects of exercise on the body and can evaluate her own work and that of others. Fred has developed an understanding of what it means to be an effective team player. She is confident in the water during swimming lessons and is developing the main strokes.

Religious Education

This year in RE we have studied Christianity and Islam. Fred has shown interest in most of the areas we have covered, including learning about religious stories, celebrations, rules and religious places. Fred can confidently identify some of the key beliefs and practices of both religions showing a good understanding and awareness of similarities and differences. She confidently takes part in group discussions to share her thoughts and is able to consider other points of view on religion, faith, ceremonies and beliefs. Fred particularly enjoyed some of the more practical activities we did this year, such as using drama to display certain religious stories. Overall, she has made good progress in her understanding of Christianity and Islam this year.

Environmental Studies Specialism

The children have been taking an active role in developing a Wildlife Garden. Through this, Fred has shown a good understanding of how to sow a range of seeds and how to plant bulbs and fully grown plants. She can use an increasing range of gardening equipment safely and with growing confidence for either planting or weeding. Fred can successfully use her scientific knowledge when discussing plants; ways in which we can encourage wildlife into our garden; why pollinators are important and can use the terms vertebrate and invertebrate when describing wildlife that we can find in the garden. She can also explain the impact of litter on the environment. Fred works with great enthusiasm in lessons and I look forward to seeing her further develop her skills in our Year 4 projects.

Foundation Subjects

Subject	Effort	Subject	Effort
Art and Design	E	History	G
Computing	E	Languages	G
Design and Technology	E	Music	G
Geography	G		

Foundation Subjects Comments

Fred has enjoyed many of the topics we have been learning this year. These topics involve skills being developed around a theme and each topic lasts half a term. In particular, Fred enjoyed our 'Imaginary Creatures' and 'Explosion and Fire' topics. During the Imaginary Creatures topic, she enjoyed writing her own story, set in an imaginary world, based on The Secrets of Droon, and liked the launch event for our Roman topic, when the Roaming Roman came in to school. Fred's favourite foundation subjects have been computing and art and she has really impressed me with some of the art she has produced this year, especially her imaginary creature. She clearly has a very enthusiastic approach to this subject and her creativity helped her a great deal when designing her imaginary creature on the computer using the Spore programme. Fred was then able to sketch her creature before making it using plasticine, adding detail and colour appropriately. Fred always tries really hard in all subjects across the curriculum and has produced many pieces of topic learning to be proud of this year.

Head Teacher:	Teacher:

Date: 13/06/2017

Prayers.

Then;

The Lord's Prayer

Our Father who art in heaven,
Hallowed be thy name.
Thy Kingdom come,
Thy will be done,
On earth as it is in heaven
Give us this day our daily bread.
And forgive us our trespasses,
As we forgive those who trespass against us.
And lead us not into temptation,
But deliver us from evil.
For thine is the kingdom, the power
And the glory.
For ever and ever.

Amen.

Now;

The Lord's Prayer

Our Father in heaven,
Hallowed be your name.
Your Kingdom come,
Your will be done,
On earth as in heaven
Give us today our daily bread.
Forgive us our sins,
As we forgive those who sin against us.
Lead us not into temptation,
But deliver us from evil.
For the kingdom,
The power and the glory are yours.
Now and for ever.

Amen.

Our School Creed

This is our school,

Let peace dwell here,

Let the rooms be full of contentment,

Let love abide here,

Love of one another,

Love of mankind,

Love of life itself and love of God.

Let us remember that,

As many hands build a house,

So many hearts make a school.

Amen

Fashion from the 1960s and 70s!

…did people really dress like that?

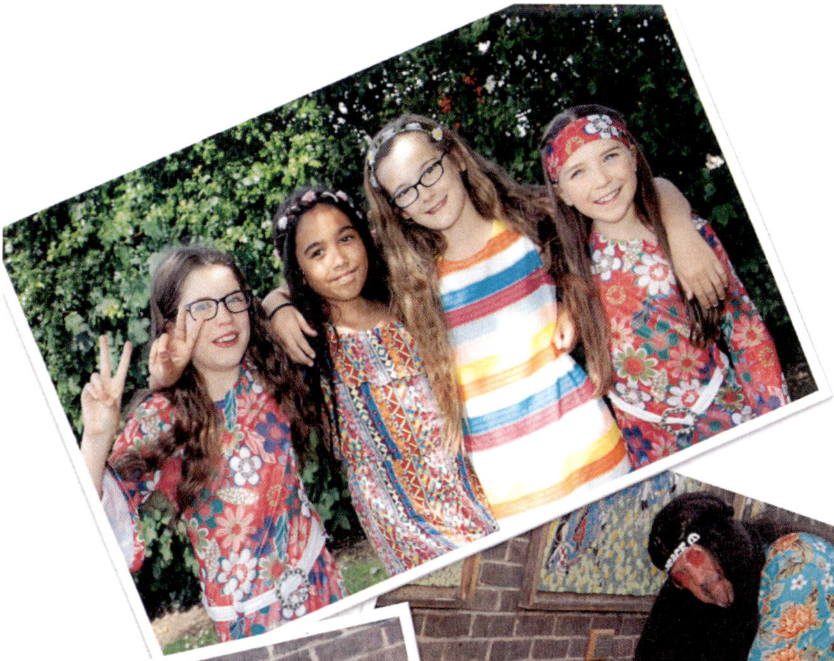

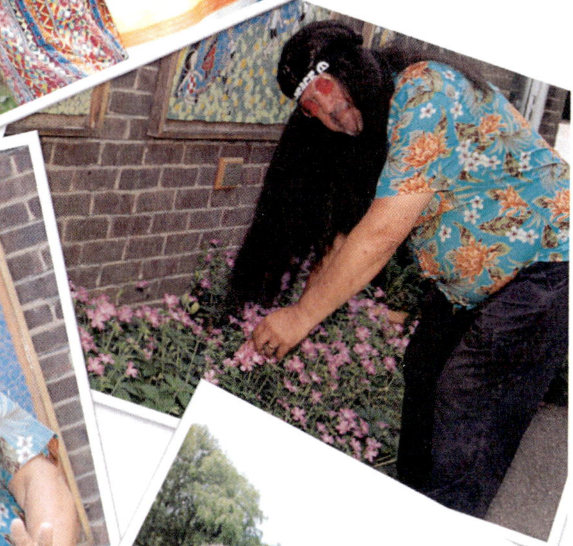

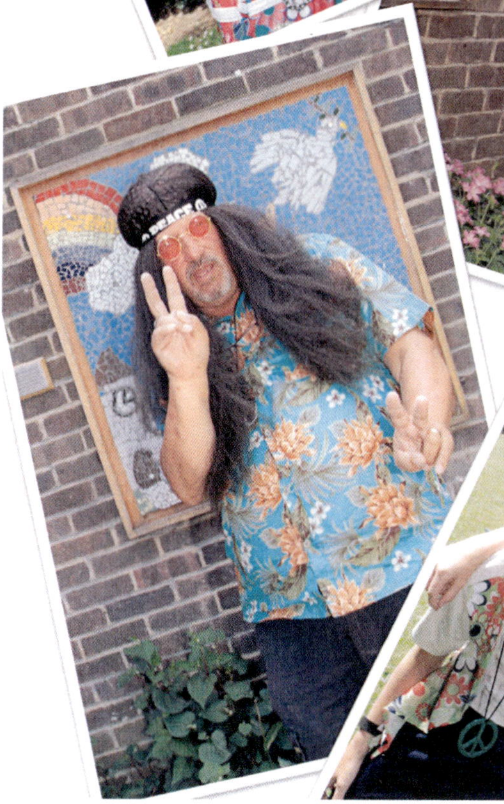
PEACE

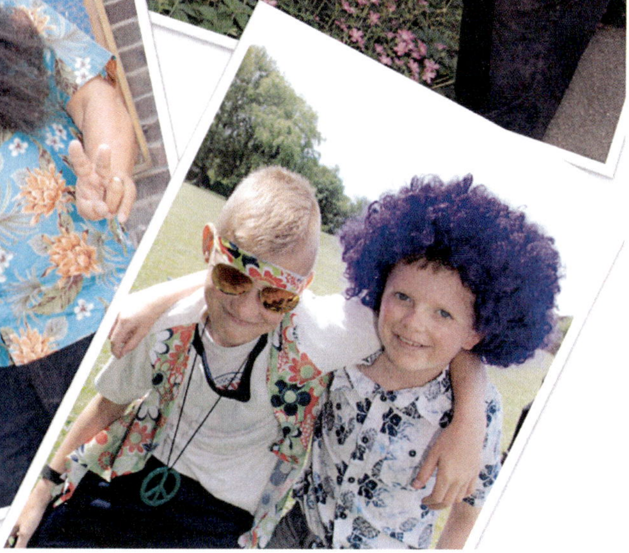

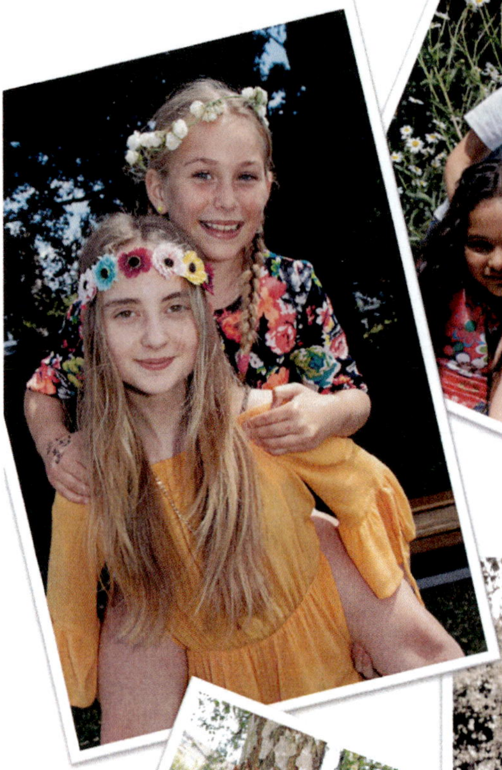

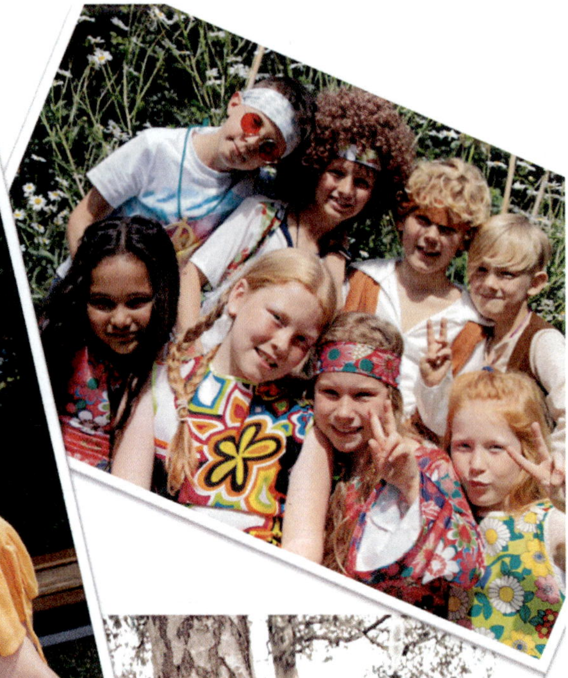

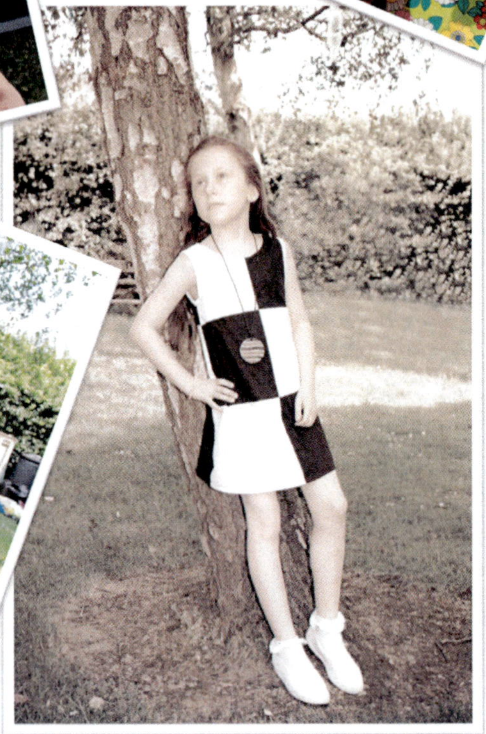

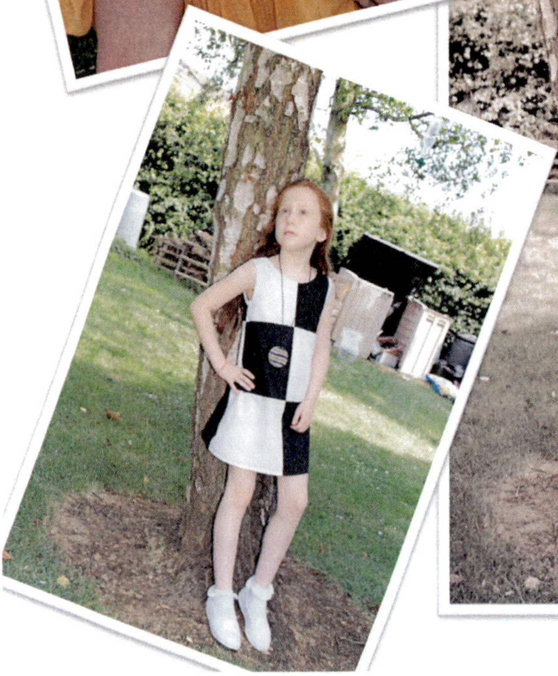

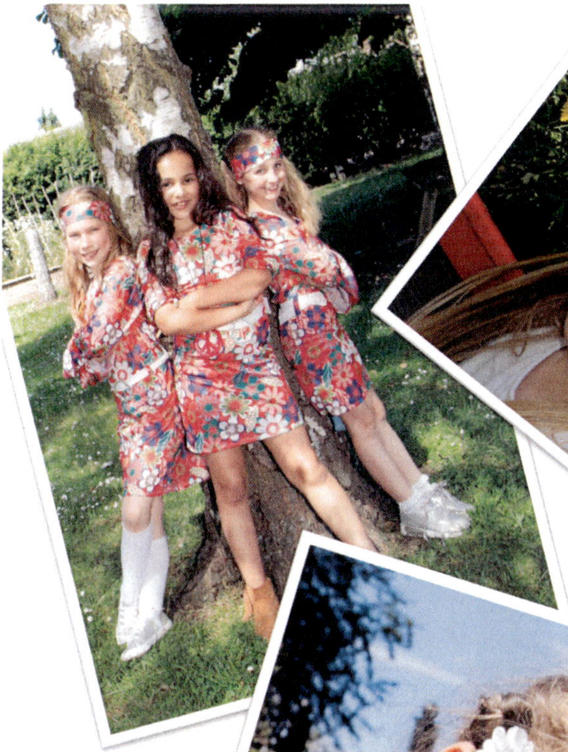
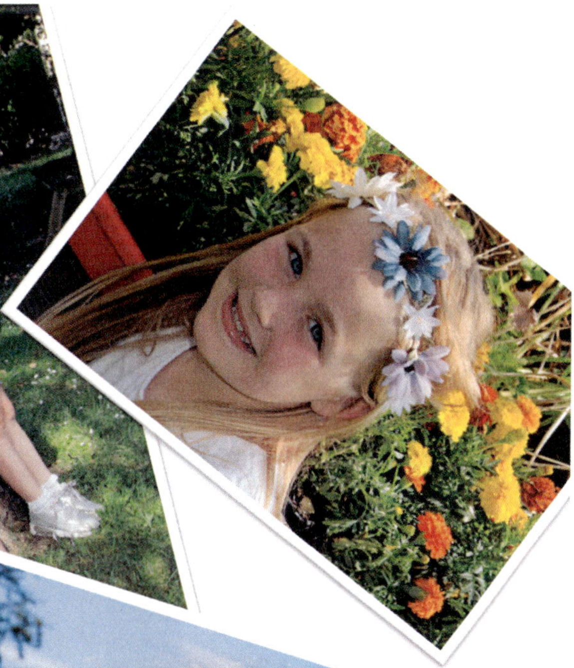
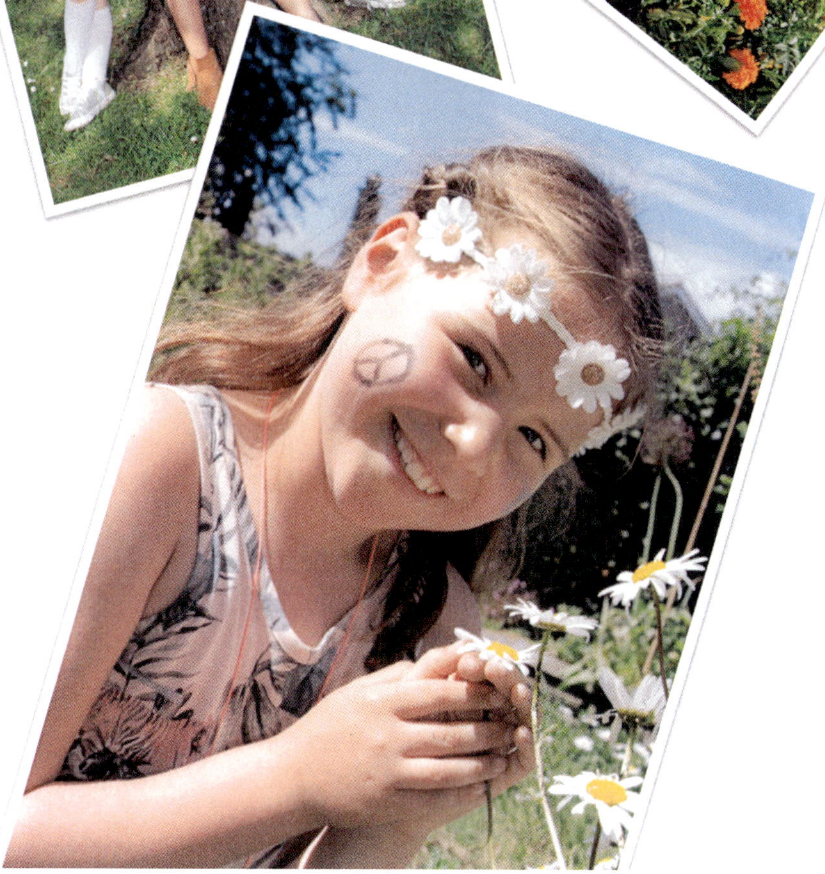

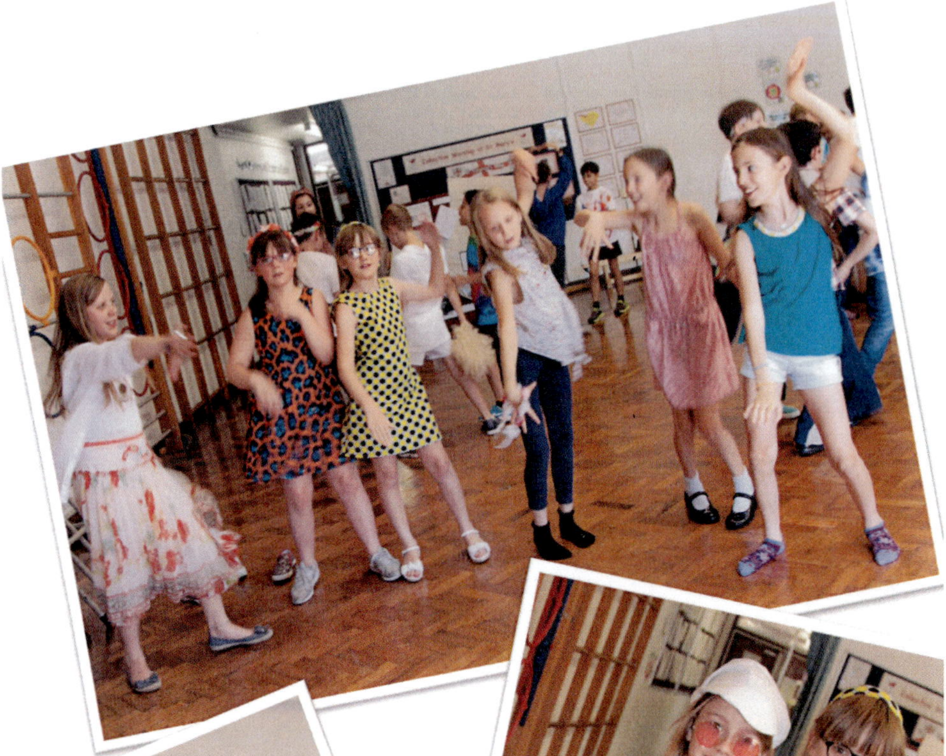

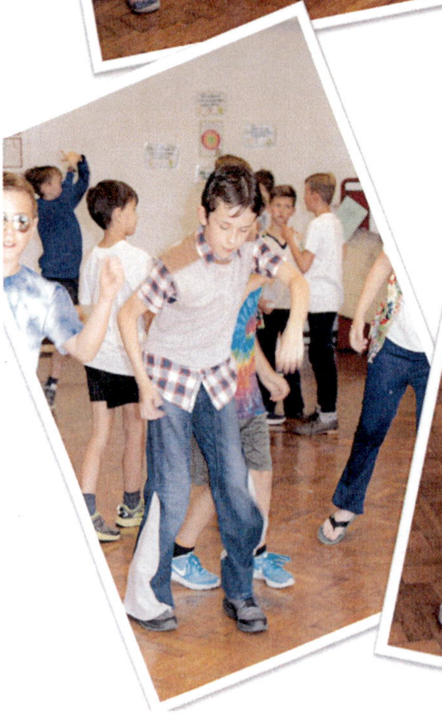

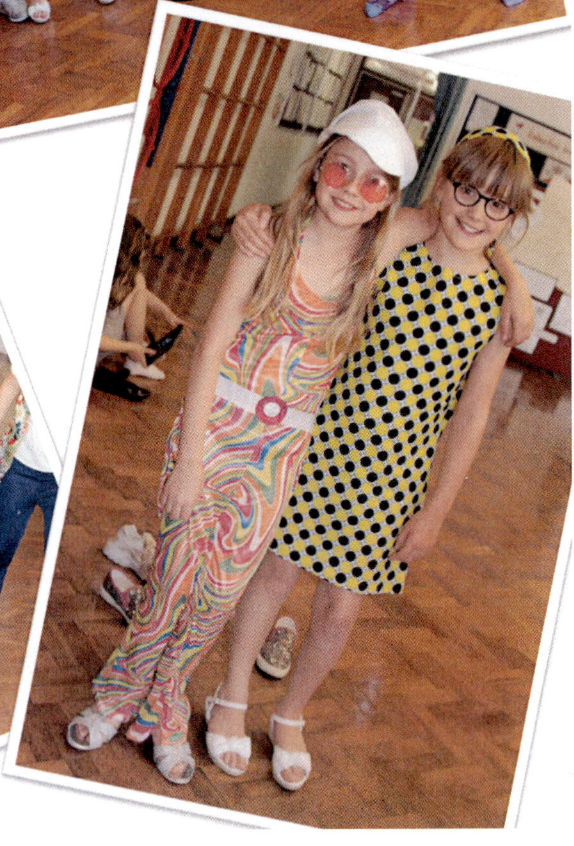

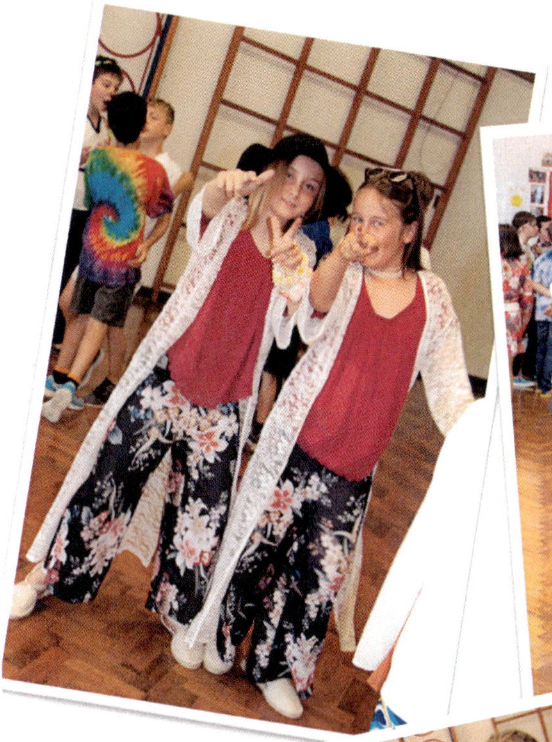

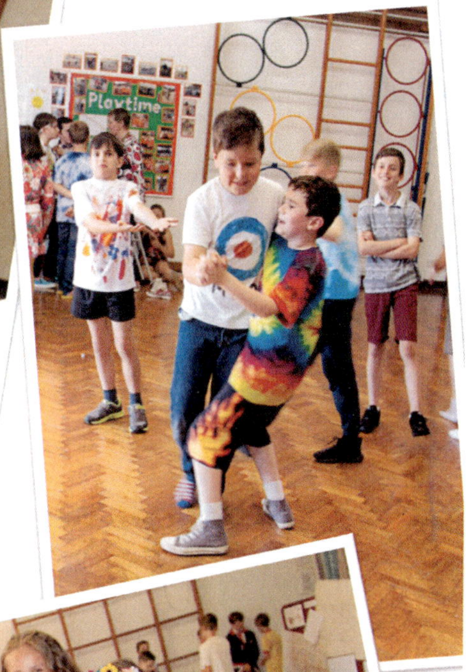
Playtime

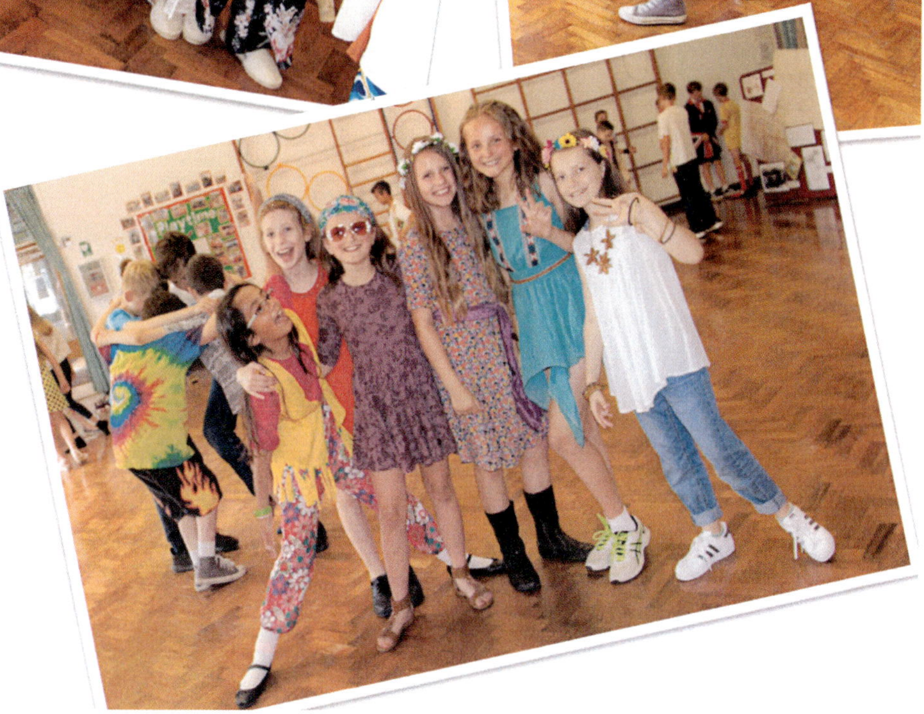

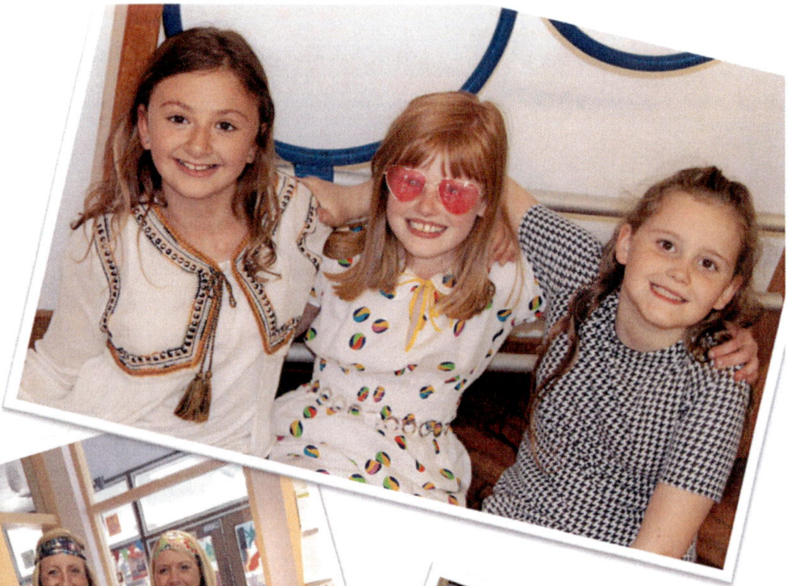

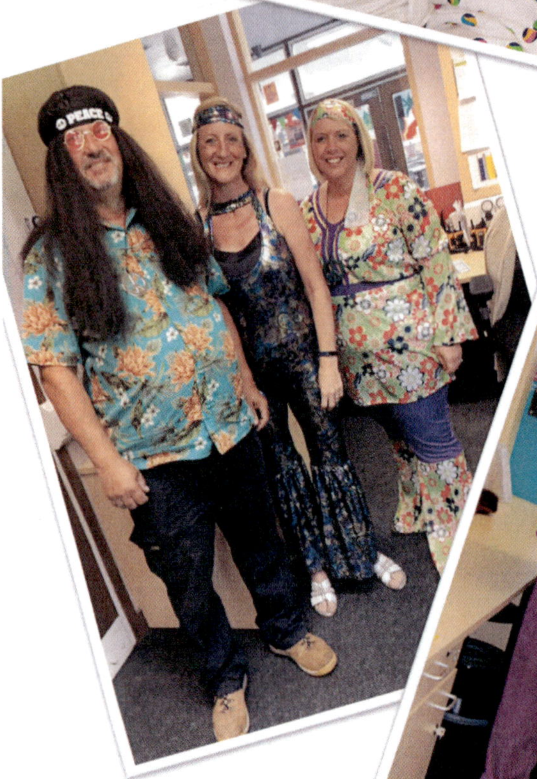
PEACE

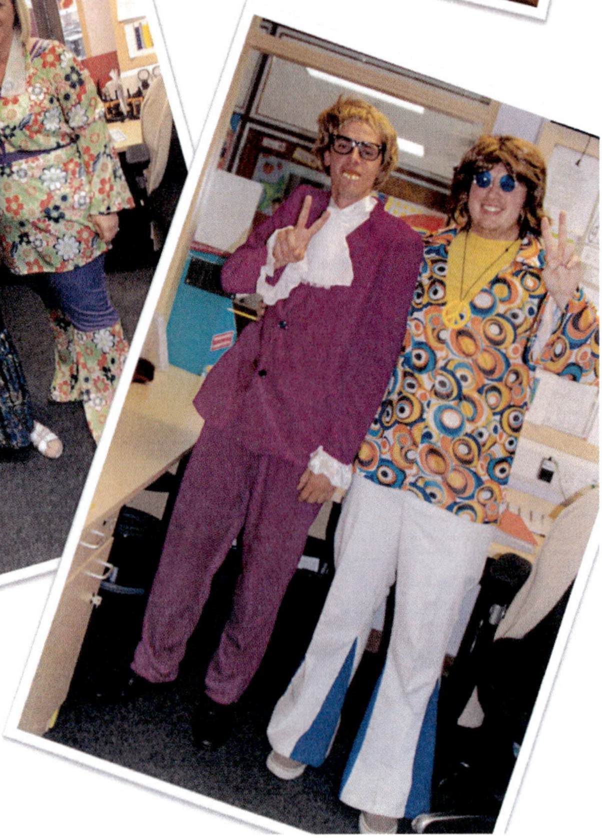

Year 3
'Letters and e-mails'

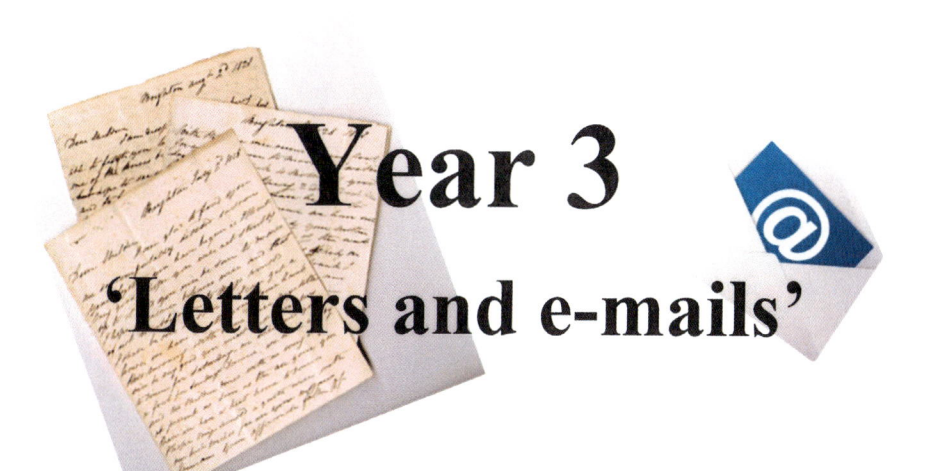

Year 3 children have had to take a step back in time to 1967 to write letters to their imaginary grandparents. Letters that had to include references to how life, including school life, might have been like in that era. The children then had to return to the present and write e-mails that reflected life in today's society. Can you spot any of the significant differences between 'Then' and 'Now'?

Mrs Bunce's Class; 3B

From left to right in both pictures.
Top row: Miss Davies, James, Billy, Harry, Kieran, Sophie, Darragh, Harrison, Jay, Samuel
Middle row: Angel, Lily-May, Niamh, Paolo, Kayla, Millie, Olivia, Mrs Bunce
Sitting: Mrs Munt, Oscar, Harry, Sam, Thomas, Gene, Bertie, Logan, Ben, Sam
Bottom row: Ilaria, Lucy, Lali, Alana

St Marys Junior school
Heath Drive
Ware
Herts
SG12 ORL

Tuesday 13th June 1967

Dear Grandma,

I hope you are well. I am writing to tell you how school is going and what I have been doing recently because I have not seen you in a while.

My favourite lesson at school is Maths because it is the only that our teacher is not very scary. I think it is because we all like maths so no one is very naughty. Luckily no one has been hit with a slipper yet! Were you ever hit with a slipper when you were at school?

After maths we normally have lunch and I absolutely hate the school meals so I walk home by myself and have lunch there. There is only one school pudding that I like which is sponge pudding. Sometimes I stay at school for lunch if that is what we are having for pudding. When I get back to school I play football with my friends. I always score lots of goals so people like to have me on their team. On some days we are allowed to go on the metal climbing frame at lunch time but I do not like it because it's very high.

Last weekend I went with my friend to the Cinema to see the Jungle Book. It was really fun because we had popcorn. But this weekend we went to the park to play football. It was nice because after—

Wards I got a chocolate ice cream.

Please write back to me. Mum and Dad send their Love.

Love From
AndrewXxx

Lali Lister, Sam shurety and Angel Campbell

Subject: Catching up

Year 3B
13.6.2017: 13:22

To: Grandad@email.co.uk

Dear Grandad,

How are you? I haven't seen you for a long time. I heard about your operation on your back. I hope you are recovering well.

I went to Italy in the half term. It was hot and sunny every day so I went swimming nearly every day. I had so much fun. We climbed some mountains which was exhausting. I went to the Leaning Tower of Pisa and I went inside and climbed to the top. There was an amazing view. Have you ever been to Italy?

At the weekend I went to our school fair. Did you ever do school fairs? Then I had a sleepover with my friend Chloe. Did you ever have sleepovers with your friends? Then on Sunday I went on a really long walk with Mum and Dad to Hertford. When we were there we stopped for a drink. I had a huge hot chocolate with cream and marshmallows. It was delicious!

At school I did a play with the rest of the class and it was about Easter and it was really fun. We also did my favourite lesson this week which is computing and we did coding. Do you know how to code? Maybe I could teach you when I next see you? I had a great week. When you were at school did you have a favourite lesson? If you did what was it?

Looking forward to your reply and please let me know how you are.

Love from
Mia

Ilaria Laudato, Paolo Daffada and Kieran Tew

St Marys Junior school
Heath Drive
Ware
SG-12 ORL
Tuesday 13th June 1967

Dear Nanny

I hope you are feeling well. I would like to tell you what I have been doing recently because I haven't seen you in two months.

On Monday I started a new school. The worst thing was that I didn't do enough work so I got hit with a slipper. My favourite lesson is maths because I love learning my times tables. I've just joined choir in my school and I got to sing lots of songs. What was your favourite lesson when you were at school?

At the weekend I went to the cinema as a special treat for doing great work at school. I went to watch Jungle Book. My favourite part of the film was when the snake trapped Mowgli in his tail. Have you seen a film lately?

The last thing I would like to tell you is that after school on Tuesday I went to my friends Amy's house. We went on a bike ride to the Priory. We had a picnic then we went back to Amy's house and played dollies until I had to go home. Do you remember the dolls clothes you made me? Please could you make some for Amy? She loves dolls as much as I do.

Please write back to me. Mum and Dad send lots of love to you.
Lots of love
Susan.

Amelia Morrison, Millie Hills Chalk and Sam Davies.

Subject: Catching up

Y3 Year 3B
13.6.2017: 13:22
To: Grandma@email.co.uk

Reply all | ∨

Dear Grandma,

Are you well? How's Grandad feeling? I am writing to you because I haven't emailed you in a long time and I thought I would let you know what I did in the summer holidays and how school is going.

I had a really fun day at school on Tuesday. Although maybe I was a bit too excited because I talked too much so Mrs Lavender told me off and I had to stay in at break. At least it was non-uniform day. I dressed up as Ginny from Harry Potter because it was World Book Day. Cool, right? Ginny is a witch and is in Gryffindor which is a house at Hogwarts. On Tuesday I also did a bake sale for World Book Day. I made cookies and iced a book on top and designed make believe animals on my cupcakes. I raised lots of money for a charity called Cancer Research UK. Have you ever been to a bake sale? You would have liked the cupcakes I made. Also on Tuesday I learnt how to make a game in computing. Did you get to go on computers when you were at school?

I am looking forward to next week because Amelia and Bertie are going to come round on Thursday. We are going to play pirates. At the weekend we are going to a swimming pool. We have been before and it was epic because there was a splash pool and I played in it and went on our lilo. Do you know how to swim? I wish you could come at the weekend. Maybe we can go swimming next time I see you?

In the summer holiday, my best friend came round and we tucked into a lovely midnight feast when Mum wasn't looking. When we woke up we watched a film while eating breakfast and then she went home. Then I played Pokémon Go and Terraria on my iPad. The next day we went on holiday to Portugal. There were lovely custard tarts and, especially as I have a sweet tooth, I loved them. In Portugal we went to the beach. We played in the water and sunbathed. Dad got really burnt but he is okay now.

I hope you will email me back soon. Did you have a nice weekend?

Lots of love
Abigail

Ben Wiggins Thomas Humphries Lucy Norris

St Mary's Junior School
Heath Drive
Ware
Herts
SG12 0RL

Tuesday 13th June 1967

Dear Grandad

I hope that you are well. I thought that I would write to you because I haven't seen you in a few months. How are you?

I thought I would write to you to tell you about what I have being doing at school. We have been learning about division in maths but I got bored so I talked to my friend. My teacher was angry so I got hit with the slipper. Did you like maths when you were at school? But other than that it was a good week because I had spam fritters and pink custard for lunch most days. I liked it alot.

Last Saturday I wanted to go to the park but my mum said I needed to tidy my room. So finally I tidied my room. Then when I had finished I went out to the park with my friend called Mark. We played football and I scored the most goals.

In the summer holidays I want my family to get a colour television so I can watch it in colour. When I was at Mark's house last week, he told me about his cousins in America who have their programmes shown in colour. I would love to be able to watch

Dr Who, in colour because it is my favourite programme.

Please write back to me so I can hear about what you have been doing recently.

Love
   from
       Richard.

James. Ambler, Sophie Jamierson
   Oscar Legrix - Hauen

Subject: Catching up

Year 3B
13.6.2017: 13:22

To: Grandpa@email.co.uk

Reply all

Dear Grandpa,

I was wondering if you were wanting to hear about my half term and what I have been doing at school.

I'm looking forward to starting computing at school next week as my teacher said we are doing coding. Additionally I got a certificate in assembly for doing well in geography this week. Did you get certificates in your school? My favourite lesson is environmental studies although earlier in the year I didn't like it but now we're planting flowers, I like it.

On Mondays we have a swimming lesson and I am practising my back stroke. Maybe we can go swimming together the next time I see you? I'm sad to say that I was talking when the teacher was writing on the board in English so I got moved down. I made sure I was good for the rest of the day. I even worked hard in maths even though it's my least favourite subject.

It has been raining a lot this week so we have had wet play at school. During wet play we played lots of fun games. My favourite board game is Snakes and Ladders. What is your favourite game?

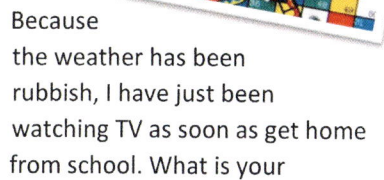

Because the weather has been rubbish, I have just been watching TV as soon as get home from school. What is your favourite TV show? My favourite shows are Tom and Jerry and The Amazing World of Gumball. In the half-term I am going round to my friend's house. We're going to have a scooter ride in the street and we are going to a trampoline park.

Looking forward to hearing from you.

Hope to see you soon.

Love from Emily

Harry Lightfoot, Lily Rose and Darragh O'Reilly

St marys Junior school
Heath Drive
Ware
Herts
SG12 0RL
Wednesday 14th June
1967

Dear Grandma,
How are you? I hope you are well. I am writing to let you know that my school has finally moved to a new site.

At the moment I am feeling a bit worried and scared because the new school is so much bigger and I may get lost. I am also excited as the playground has a field which looks like fun.

At Break time on the first day I went outside to play on the metal climbing frame and used the little house. Then break time was over so I went inside to get changed for P.E.. What was your favourite piece of equipment when you were at school? After P.E. we went inside to do English.

Next it was lunch time so we went into the dining hall where I had spam fritters and pink custard which are my favourites, yum yum. Do you ever eat pink custard? You should try if you haven't. After lunch I went outside but it was raining so I came back in and played with the wooden trains and cars. Then lunch time was

Over So it was double maths which is my least favourite subject. Finally it was home time.

At the weekend Mum and Dad took us to the cinema to watch the new James Bond flim we had popcorn and a vanilla milkshake. After the cinema I went home and went to bed. I had had a really busy week at my new school so I was really tired. I hope you are well grandma and I hope to see you soon.
love
 from
  William

Harry Hatton, Alana Hammond, Billy Batts

Subject: Catching up

Year 3B
13.6.2017: 13:22
To: Grandad@email.co.uk

Reply all

Dear Grandad,

How are you? I heard that you started playing bowls again. I am assuming this means that your back is better? I haven't emailed you in a while so I thought I would talk to you about how I am doing in school and what I did in my half-term.

In our computing lessons we are doing coding. I'm so excited because I love coding so much. Did you do coding when you were at school? In art we have been making pots with clay. It was very hard but it was worth it because it came out beautiful. I can't wait to paint it.

In my half-term I went to an all day football club. It was so fun. Did you play football when you were young? On Sunday Mia and I made a water slide and played in it. It was so fun because we have a hill in our garden so we slide so fast down the hill. Tonight I'm going to Cubs and we are going to make a fire. I hope I don't burn myself while toasting marshmallows! Did you go to Cubs when you were young?

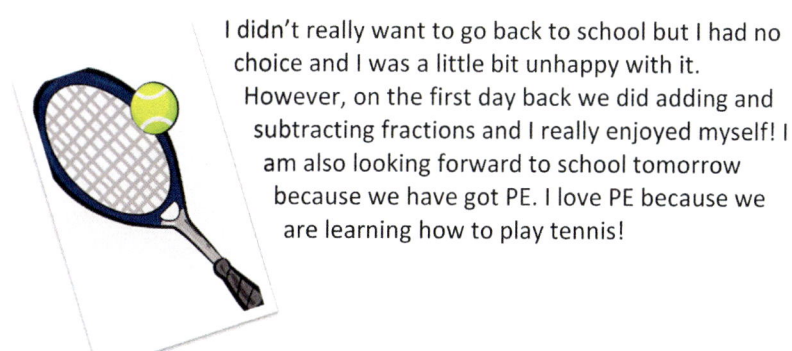

I didn't really want to go back to school but I had no choice and I was a little bit unhappy with it. However, on the first day back we did adding and subtracting fractions and I really enjoyed myself! I am also looking forward to school tomorrow because we have got PE. I love PE because we are learning how to play tennis!

I hope you reply soon and I can't wait to see you again. I was thinking we could go out for lunch the next time I see you.

Love from
Leo

Olivia Watson, Logan Bridgeman and Gene Tierney

St. Marys Junior School
Heath Drive
Ware
Herts
SG12 0RL

Tuesday 13th June 1967

Dear Grandma

How are you? I wanted to write to you because I haven't seen you in ages. How was your birthday? I hope you had a lovely day.

At school I am studying maths, English, dance and nature studies. My favourite subject is English because we write stories. My least favourite subject is maths because I sometimes get hit with the slipper. Did you get hit with the slipper when you were young?

We are doing a leavers play before we go to secondary school. The play is called The Night Sky and I am playing the moon which is one of the main characters. If I act well mum says I can have pink custard and sponge pudding after the play. Do you like pink custard?

My favourite day of the week is Tuesday because my friend Susan comes round my house and we play hopscotch. I am really good at hopscotch. Did you play hopscotch when you were young?

Please reply to my letter and all of my family sends their love.

Love from Julie

Sam Gore, Niamh O'Shea and Jay Fotheringham

Subject: Catching up

Year 3B

13.6.2017: 13:22

To: Grandad@email.co.uk

Reply all | ∨

Dear Grandad,

How are you? I'm writing to you because I thought you would like to hear about how I am getting on at school. Is your leg better? I heard that you had an operation on it.

I am really excited about school at the moment because we are doing coding on the computers and researching about the 1960s music, TV programmes and fashion. We found out that you only had three channels! What was it like with just three channels? Also this week I have been learning different spelling patterns and I made a smooth clay pot in art.

In half term I went to a massive waterpark with Mum and Dad. There was a huge swimming pool and we really got wet! On Wednesday we went back home and the car journey was really boring.

At the weekend I went on a playdate with my friends Josh and Henry. On Sunday we went to the sweet shop to spend our pocket money on sweets and chocolate. After that we went home and watched TV. We watched Dr Who and it was really fun to watch. Did you watch Dr Who when you were little? Who was the Doctor Who when you were little?

I hope to hear from you soon!

Love from Oliver

Bertie Stevens, Kayla Storey and Harrison Eglin

Mr Martin's Class; 3M

From left to right in both pictures.
Top row: Miss Stagg, Jake, Cameron, Sophie, Demii, Emily, Mason, Joe, Mr Martin
Middle row: Jay Jay, Morgan, Anya, Mimi, Zak, Finley, Lenny, Libby, Ella, Patrick
Sitting: Lily, Summer, Alice, Freddie, Zach, Joe, Lexi, Daisy, Megan
Bottom row: Finley, Charlie, Oscar

St. Mary's Junior School
Ware
Hertfordshire
SG12 0RL

Tuesday 13th June 2017

Dear Grandfather,

Hi, I haven't heard from you in a while! I would like to tell you some facts about now (1967) that you might not know!

I want to watch more channels (on my new TV that shows programmes in colour) but I can't because there are only 3 channels. Have you got a TV? The programmes that I know of are Doctor Who and Batman. The channels that there are are ITV, BBC1 and BBC2. Can you maybe tell me some new programmes?

I have just started a new school on weekends and Sundays. If you get into trouble you get the slipper thrown at you and if you get into huge trouble you will get wacked by the CANE! The lessons in school are: art, maths, English, Science and P.E. We have a desk with a lid where we have to store all of our stuff.

My mum takes me to school in a vehicle usually it's a car called a "Ford Anglia". There are other vehicles too like another car called "The Morris Minor". The other day I went in a plane that had fully powered jet engines!

I wanted to ask you some questions about now (1967) that you might just know the answer to!

Question: 1. Have you heard the new song by "The Beach Boys"?

Question: 2. Did you know that "The Beatles" have just released Sgt. Peppers Lonely Hearts Club in America?

Question: 3. Did you know that "The Beatles" are famous for their music but have been in a few films?

Did you think the facts are cool?
I hope you did! Please reply within the next month!
Hope you enjoyed the facts!

Love From Jane ♥Xx
(Written by Demii Haynes, Finley Dewar and Zak Taylor.)

Subject: Catching up

Year 3M
13.6.2017: 13:22
To: Nanny@email.co.uk

Reply all

Dear Nanny,

    I am writing to tell you about what is going on in my life. It has been a good life so far.

    I joined a sports club in school. They have a couple of sports. There are two sports that I like that are sprinting and javelin. We practice with foam javelins because if we used a real one it could kill someone. They are also very heavy and very dangerous.

We have a new PE teacher and she is teaching us. We do a lap of the field and we also do a warm up. Everyone gets worn out after the lap and we do cross country. Right now we are doing tennis. I am very good at tennis. My teacher got a group of us and filmed me on an iPad!

I have watched two movies over the weekend. I watched two films because I was bored. The two movies that I watched were Boss Baby and Kung Fu Panda 2. It was very funny because Kung Fu Panda 2 was very big. It was 3D and you wear 3D glasses. You wear 3D glasses so it looks like everything is coming out of the screen. In Kung Fu Panda 2 I thought it was going to kick me in the face. Boss Baby was very weird because it was a baby who talked and he was the boss of the house.

Are you going to watch the new Kung Fu Panda movie?

Do you know the new things we do in PE like javelin and sprinting?

Say hi to Grandad for me. See you soon and I hope you reply.

                    Love from,

                      Noah

(Written by Mason Wilkinson, Lennie Ballard and Megan Bray)

St Mary's Junior School,
Ware,
Herts,
SG12 ORL,

Tuesday 13th June 1967

Dear Nan,

Hello how are you? I thought I would write to you about what has been going on recently.

We finally got a TV. Have you got one yet? Sadly there are only 3 TV channels BBC1, BBC2 and Itv. Have you seen this new TV programme called Dr. Who? Some of the episodes are a bit scary. Sadly it is black and white but some programmes are in colour.

I have recently moved to a new school, I have 2 break times both for 20 minutes and 1 lunch time for an hour. Most days I have to make up my own games but some days I can play with the skipping ropes, hula hoops and the stilts. How long were your break times?

In lessons we have single desks that open for storage but when the lid is closed we have to work on it. We put a pencil sharpener, a pencil, a rubber and sometimes a pencil case in it. What did you have when you were young? How many lessons did you have a day?

I hope you will reply to me and I will see you soon
Love from
Karen xxx

(written by Alice Jancock, Charlie Mansfield and Sophie Hall)

Subject: Catching up

Year 3M
13.6.2017: 13:22
To: Nan@email.co.uk

Reply all | ˅

Dear Nan,

I'm writing to tell you about what's going on because I haven't seen you in a while.

I have just started at a new school it is called St Mary's Junior School.

There are long tables in the classroom, a big screen and whiteboards. On Mondays, Tuesdays and Thursdays we get 2 breaks, one in the morning and one in the afternoon. Now at lunch we get a sandwich option. In school, if we're naughty we get moved down on the zone board and if you get moved down again you go to the head teacher. What was it like when you were at school? Did you get a punishment?

In the cinema the most recent films are Beauty and the Beast, Sing, Moana, and Boss Baby. The other day my Mum took me to the cinema for a treat to see Sing. My favourite movie is Moana, it was in 3D and we had to wear 3D glasses so it looks like it is coming out of the screen. Did you go to the cinema?

The latest fashion for girls are JOJO bows, they are big bows and for boys it is cool to wear a fitbit. They are bracelets that tell you the time and how many steps you have done. The other day Mum and I went to Claire's and bought a JOJO bow and it is yellow with diamonds on. The boys in my class are all wearing NY Yankee baseball caps and huarache trainers. They think they look really cool! What did people wear when you were younger?

I hope you are well and would love to hear back from you soon.

                Love from,

                Olivia xxx

(Written by Emily McCutcheon, Summer Scripps and Jake Parker)

St. Mary's Junior School
Ware
Hertfordshire
SG12 0RL
Tuesday 13th June 1967

Dear Nan,
    I'm writing to tell you about the new things that are coming out. Would you like to hear?

Have you seen the new fashion? Mary Quant and flower power are the most popular. Flower power has flower up and down the dress, Mary Quant has black and white chequered dress. Men wear suits and grey jumpers, black trousers and velvet cap.

    I'm waiting for the new colour tv to come out. I wonder what the new colour tv will be like? Have you watched Animal Magic, if not its on Itv.

When I started school I didn't know that you had to buy dinner tickets, I neary didnt have dinner! My favourite game at school is two ball, you throw and catch up a wall, if you have not tried this game you should try it.

I wonder what the fashion will be in the future? Have got the new colour tv? I hope you write back to me.

From
Jane xx
xx

(Written by Alexis Walker, Ella Read and Cameron Taylor)

Subject: Catching up

Year 3M

13.6.2017: 13:22

To: Grandad@email.co.uk

Reply all | ⌄

Dear Grandad,

    I thought I should write to you because I haven't seen you in a while.

I now have more teddies because it's been my birthday recently and I got loads of new toys. One of them is a Beanie Boo. It is a teddy that is quite small and has large eyes. It's black and has white fangs and with multi-coloured wings. I have a white Build-A-Bear. I was also given a bunny that is my favourite and it's blue and fluffy. I also have a rainbow fidget spinner. It is a toy that you can spin and comes in many colours. Has Grandma bought you a fidget spinner yet? My favourite thing to do is to make unicorn slime. You put sparkles or sequins in the slime and then fold it in. Have you made slime?

I have this bow called a jojo bow. It is a big bow that comes in any colour and is the latest fashion. I love playsuits but on holiday I wear earrings and crop tops. I wear high heels for special occasions. I bought these when my brother was playing football. Claire's is my favourite place to get accessories. I have a necklace that has pearls on. Has Grandma been to Claire's? I also wear Claire's dresses and playsuits. My favourite playsuit colour is navy blue.

Have you seen Britain's Got Talent? It is when people go on stage and show their talent. Have you seen Strictly Come Dancing? On the latest episode Bruno fell off of his chair. I went to see Boss Baby with my mum and dad. Have you seen Boss Baby? I also saw Dog Days which is a Diary of the Wimpy Kid film. There's a boy called Greg and his dad's called Frank, his older brother is called Rodrick and his baby brother is called Manny. The dad buys a dog called Sweetie but Rodrick gets a dog bowl that says Sweaty on it.

I feel much better after talking to you and looking forward to your reply. Please say hello to Grandma.

I love you lots,

Emma

XXX

(Written by Mimi Whetstone, Lily North and Joe Southwell)

St Mary's Junior School,
Ware,
Hertfordshire
SG12 OBL
Tuesday 13th June 1967

Dear Nan,
 I thought I would write to you because I haven't spoken to you in a while.

I love playing twister. I got it for my birthday. Have you ever played twister? It's better then my wooden toys and dolls. Kerplunk is the newest game out. It looks really fun to play with. I hope to get it for Christmas. Also I have loads of board games. What's your favourite board game?

I got a mini skirt and a flowert-shirt. I got it for my disco. They go perfectly together. It's the latest trend. All the girls wear it. The boys wear flares and a flared t-shirt. The favourite patterns on my clothes are swirls and flowers. I like bright colours on my clothes because it makes me look groovy!

My record collection is getting bigger. I now have Elvis Presley, The Monkeys, The Beach Boys, The Beatles and Aretha Franklin. My favourite song is Respect by Aretha Franklin, it's second in the charts in America. I dance round my room and listen to it every evening. Have you heard the latest Beach Boys song?

Who is your favourite singer?

I hope you are well. It would be great if you could write back soon and let me know how you are. I look forward to hearing from you.

lots of love
Tracey xxx ♡

(Written by Anya Pettit, Daisy Nippard and Patrick Raynham)

Subject: Catching up

Year 3M
13.6.2017: 13:22
To: Grandma@email.co.uk

Dear Grandma,

    I haven't seen you in a long time so I thought I would write to you. I am writing to tell you about the toys, buildings and movies that have come out recently.

It was my birthday recently, so thank you for the money you gave me because I spent some on a fidget spinner. It is a toy to keep you entertained. I also got a new X-Box One from Dad, some coloured paper for my origami, and a giant box of Lego! So far I have made a house bigger than me. Have you got a new fidget spinner?

Next week I am going to the cinema with my friends to watch the Lion King or the new Despicable Me film in 3D. To make it look 3D you need to put special glasses on to make it look like it is coming right at you. Have you seen one of those?

I am going on holiday soon to Dubai and going up the Burj Khalifa building. Did you know it is the tallest building in the world? It is 828m high! Have you gone on holiday this year? Have you heard about The Shard in London, have you been to it? As we are talking about buildings, our swimming pool has just been redecorated at school, they have made the floor smoother so we don't cut our feet. It also looks better now it has been refurbished.

I hope you are well. I miss you. Please write back to me soon. Please say hello to Grandad.

Love from,

Oscar

(Written by Oscar Shaikh, Joe Munt and Freddy Gladding)

ST Mary's Junior School,
Ware,
Hertfordshire
SG12 0RL
Tuesday 13th June
1967

Dear Nan,

I am writing to find out about films, TV shows and channels. Nan maybe I could come to yours to see the new TV shows. Are there any other channels except ITV? I've heard that there are others called BBC 1 and the BBC 2. Have you seen the new Addams family it came out last week also Batman and Doctor Who? I would love for you to tell me channels. I'm looking for channels in colour.

Can you tell me funny films? Doctor Dolittle was my favourite.

Can you tell me the kids films? I've been watching Doctor Dolittle again and again. Have you seen the Jungle Book and Doctor Dolittle?

What are the TV shows that you think I will like?

Do you think there are channels that you think Mum and Dad will like?

I've just joined a new school and the lessons are different when you were a kid when you were Punished did you get hit by the cane or the slipper? The breaks are really short they're about two minutes It must have been longer for you. But it doesn't feel like it for me.

I hope you are well and say hello to grandad for me. Lots of love, Richard
(Written by Dominic Hacking, Morgan Frost-Feary and Zach Levy.)

Subject: Catching up

Year 3M
13.6.2017: 13:22
To: Grandad@email.co.uk

To Grandad,

I haven't heard from you in a while so I'm writing to tell you about the P.E. in school, sports around the world and movies. What have you been up to?

I've got into the athletics club at school and I have learned how to throw a ball extremely far, I have improved on my sprinting and I can jump 2.5 meters. I was also using foam javelins and I threw it 10 meters. Last week it was cross country and I came 1st. In school they have opened a new basketball club and it is really good. You should try basketball sometime. I found that I'm a really good defender in hockey because I only let two goals in my team and won 10-2. My teacher filmed me to be used as an example. Everyone on my team was cheering for me! Have you ever thrown a foam javelin? How fast can you run?

It's been half term and Dad took me to see the Guardians of the Galaxy. It is a film and I think that it's brilliant I also got the songs out of It think you should definitely watch it. It's about people who kill bad guys. The film Boss Baby is about a baby a boss is really good and everyone has seen it. I watched it in 3D. 3D is when you wear these special glasses and it looks like you're in the film. What's your favourite film?

There are loads of sports that I follow. Football is my favourite sport and Chelsea came 1st in the Premier League and Spurs came 2nd with Liverpool in 3rd place. In the Six Nations (rugby) it was France against Scotland and France won 22-16. It was also Scotland against Wales and Scotland won 29-13. These are the top three people in the latest golf tournament, the U.S. Open: Brooks Koepka came 1st and Hideki Matsuyama and Brian Harman came joint second. Have you ever been on a golf course?

I hope you are ok and I'm looking forward to your reply.

Love from,

Reggie

(Written by Finley Haylock, Jay-Jay Baylis and Libby Walker)

Year 4
'School life in 1967 and today'

Year 4 children have written comparative reports based on their research of what school life would have been like in 1967 compared to their experiences in school today. The children have considered the evidence to help support their opinions and preferences. What would your view be?

Mr Cox's Class; 4C

From left to right in both pictures.
Top row: Leia, Maisey, Alf, Mr Cox, Alfie, Jasmin, Hollie
Middle row: Tillie, Ben, Jaidan, Jayley, Imogen, Lila, Charlie, Clarice
Sitting: Jayden, Sarah, Haakon, Ella, Ollie, Lily, Lennon, Laura, Daniel
Bottom row: Annabella, Bradley, Mia-Rose, Max, Ruby, Jaz

Comparing School Life in 1967 and Today

School life in 1967

In 1967 school life was quite different. If you did something extremely bad you got a violent punishment called corporal punishment. You usually got hit by a hard, wooden ruler or caned. Secondly, the lunches were also very different because they only allowed school dinners and you only got one choice. If the children didn't eat everything they wouldn't be allowed out. They sat in rows and their desks had lids for storage. The blackboard rolled down so you didn't have to wipe it. They also had a cute, fluffy school pet. The teachers could teach whatever they wanted to. In the morning, the teachers would usually put on the radio and the kids would have books and they could sing along to it.

School life in 2017

Although, some things are the same, many aspects of school life have changed in 2017. For school dinners there is now a bigger variety of choice and you now don't have to eat everything. You also don't have to have school dinners. Now, you don't have storage in your desks, we have trays and lockers instead. You have whiteboards instead of blackboards. You don't have corporal punishment anymore, instead you get punished by staying inside, finishing work or doing lines. Instead of getting caned you have to talk to the head teacher about what you've done. The teachers have to follow a curriculum and now can't teach what they want to.

Our Opinions

We have managed to find some things we like about schools fifty years ago and some things we like about schools today. We liked the idea that they had a class pet. We also like the idea that the teachers could teach whatever they wanted to. In 2017, we like the school dinners and the electronics.

Max-"I would prefer to go to school in 2017 because you wouldn't get caned and 1967 because you could have a class pet."

Laura-"I would prefer to go to school in 2017 because I don't like the idea of corporal punishment."

Laura Bassom and Max Woodward

Comparing School Life in 1967 and Today

School Life in 1967

In 1967 school life was quite different. Often when the children had lunch they used to be forced to eat everything served on their plate. When the children were being taught they watched telly programmes to learn things. When the teachers taught the children they could choose what to teach. When the children were naughty they would get told off or get whacked with the cane. The children would only get smacked with the headteacher's cane if they were extremely naughty. Otherwise they would be smacked bare handed. 1967's class layout were in long, straight rows of desks facing the front. Also there was a space inside the desks where the children kept their books.

School Life in 2017

Although some things are the same, many aspects of school life have changed in 2017. When you go in to lunch you can now choose anything from the hatch and you don't have to eat everything. In 2017 we have wooden tables which have metal legs. Often, the tables have six places where the children can sit while doing their work. 2017's punishment is very different from 1967's, you won't be smacked by the teacher. You also won't be smacked with the cane, you would only get a telling off. Nowadays the teachers would be told what to teach by the Government. Today the teachers do the teaching therefore a radio is not needed.

Our Opinions

We have managed to find some things we like about schools fifty years ago and some things we like about schools today. We like that you did not have to wear a school uniform in 1967. We like that you can choose what lunches you have in 2017 as well as not having corporal punishment.

Jaz- "I would prefer to go to school in 2017 because people won't be hit by the teacher's cane and you don't have to eat everything on your plate."

Ben- "I would prefer to go to school in 2017 because we have technology. For example an iPad."

Ben Murphy and Jaz Capel-Maniam

Comparing School Life in 1967 and Today

School Life in 1967

In 1967 school life was quite different. Surprisingly, the desks were laid in straight rows facing the front. The teachers had blackboards instead of whiteboards or interactive whiteboards. Some classes had class pets. For school dinners, the children had to eat all their dinner before they were allowed to go outside whether they liked it or not. There were table heads in some schools to check that the other people on their table ate all their food and if they didn't the table heads had to eat all the leftovers. Unbelievably, instead of the government telling the teachers what to teach, the teachers could teach whatever they liked. If the teacher came in and said to write a story about a magic, shiny plate the children would just start writing. The corporal punishment at lots of schools was the cane. If you did something that wasn't so bad you wouldn't get hit, but if you did something very bad you would definitely get the cane. When you get the cane you get hit somewhere on your body with a hard, wooden ruler!

School Life in 2017

Although some things are the same, many aspects of school life have changed in 2017. Surprisingly, the lunches have changed quite a lot. There are three options for lunch: a vegetarian option, a school hot or cold option or a packed lunch from home. Nowadays you don't have to eat all your lunch so if you don't like it you don't have to eat it. Also, you don't get the cane anymore, you get sent to the headmaster or moved on to a warning. Now the classrooms are different. Desks are laid out together with six people sitting at each of them. We also have interactive-whiteboards connected to the computer so we can type our writing up. Instead of getting dirty with the chalk dust, the computers keeps us as clean as silk. Now the government tells teachers what to teach so most schools do the same things. It used to be unusual to get homework in infant or junior school. Usually, you started getting homework in secondary school but now you get homework in infants. Today in our playgrounds we have adventure playgrounds to play on.

Our Opinions

We have managed to find some things we like about schools 50 years ago and some things we like about schools today. In 1967 we like when you get lunches, some of the lunches were horrible. They could get used to the food the don't like and they get nice puddings to eat. You would get a nice lunch if your cook is nice. We also like that you have class pets so if you don't have one you can take it home. Today we like that you get a hot or cold option at school for dinners. We also like that you get discos and fun school trips.

Lily-"I would prefer to go to school in 2017 because we can pick if we get hot or cold option"

Ollie-"I would prefer to go to school in 2017 because I don't think the corporal punishment is fair because when someone doesn't own up to something naughty everyone gets the cane or the ruler and it's not fair if you didn't do it."

Ollie Dickson and Lily Mack

Comparing School Life in 1967 and Today

School life in 1967

In 1967 school life was quite different. Firstly, the desks were facing the front. There were two people per table. They had blackboards. The curriculum was very different too. They didn't have one! Teachers taught the class whatever they liked. The rule with the lunches was you had to eat it all before you went outside. In some schools there was a duty that on your table you had to eat all the disgusting, horrible leftovers. If you were naughty in class you would get hit by a cane or a ruler, this was called corporal punishment. When you were really naughty you would be sent to the head teacher's office and get caned there.

School life in 2017

Although some things are the same, many aspects of school life have changed in 2017. The curriculum is now stricter about what you need to learn, so if you go to a different school you will have learnt the same things. The classroom's layout and equipment are different. Nowadays the desks aren't in rows. They are only in rows for tests. Thanks to technology we have interactive whiteboards that are connected to computers. With the lunches you now have a lot more choice. You can have hot, cold or home lunches. Finally, corporal punishment is now not allowed to be used. If a teacher does use it they will be sacked! You also get homework, in 1967 you normally didn't until secondary school.

Our Opinions

We have managed to find some things we like about school 50 years ago and some things we like about school today. We like that teachers used corporal punishment because children would behave. In 1967 they also had class pets which we think is a good idea. Now we are glad that we get lunch choices. We also have got lots of technology. Finally, the cameras take coloured photos which is good.

Haakon-"I would prefer to go to school in 2017 because of the fun, amazing technology."

Sarah- "I would prefer to go to school in 1967 because children would be better behaved."

Sarah Preston and Haakon Tveit

Comparing School Life in 1967 and Today

School Life in 1967

In 1967, school life was quite different. The teachers didn't get told what to do by the government, they did what they wanted to do. The teachers didn't really teach, they put the children in front of a TV or a radio and they learnt from it. Also with the lunches you had to eat everything on your plate that the cooks gave you but if you were a vegetarian, you wouldn't have to eat it. Another thing is the school staff went around checking everyone had eaten everything. Some schools had duties which would seem cruel today. Also, the class layout and equipment was different. The children sat in long, cramped rows at desks which had tops that you pulled up and got their books from in the desks. The children called the male teachers 'Sir' and the female teachers 'Miss'. In schools, punishment was different. If you were naughty, you may have got hit with a ruler by a teacher or got hit by the headmaster's cane.

School life in 2017

Although some things are the same, many aspects of school life have changed in 2017. The class layout and equipment has changed. Now, we have big, shiny interactive whiteboards and the teachers' computers are connected to them. We now have air conditioning and iPads in classrooms and children now have their own lockers and drawers. We now sit in tables of six. We use iPads and computers because they are entertaining and you can learn from them without knowing. Punishment has changed in 2017. Now, you get sent to the headmaster's office or the corridor and miss a lunch or a break. Another thing that's changed is the lunches. In modern schools, you don't have to eat everything on your plate and you can bring in a packed lunch from home. You now have options for everyone, not just one choice. The curriculum is very different. Now the government tells the teachers what to do.

Our Opinions

We have to managed find some things we like about schools 50 years ago and some things we like about schools today. We like that in 1967 you would get the cane or ruler as a punishment and it was fair because if you were naughty and you just got a talking to the person could keep on doing it. We also like that in schools now you don't have to eat everything on your plate and we like the discos that we have now. We also like the new electronics because they are entertaining.

Lennon-"I would prefer to stay in 2017 because I wouldn't like to be forced to eat everything on my plate."

Bradley-"I can't choose which I would rather go to, 1967 or 2017. I couldn't choose because I agree with the Headmaster's cane but I like the homework now."

Brad Lippiatt and Lennon Corbett

Comparing School Life in 1967 and Today

School Life in 1967

In 1967 school life was quite different. Children's desks were apart and facing forwards. They were cramped all together. The curriculum was also different. Instead of a teacher having a curriculum they taught what they wanted to. Instead of a teacher teaching at the start of lessons they turned on the class' TV and the children were supposed to learn from the TV. When they did singing lessons the teacher turned on a radio. The radio presenter told you what page to sing from in the students' books. The lunches were different. You didn't have a choice, however if you were a vegetarian or allergic to something you didn't have to eat it. You had to eat all your food or you weren't allowed out to play. Corporal punishment was used when children did something naughty. They would get whacked on the hand with a ruler or if they were really naughty they would get hit with a cane.

School Life in 2017

Although some things are the same, many aspects of school life have changed in 2017. Firstly, teachers have interactive white boards. Secondly, children sit in tables of six. The lunches are different as you do have a choice of what to eat and you are not forced to eat everything on your plate. In 2017 when you get in trouble you are sent to see the head teacher and you miss break or lunch time. If you are in big trouble you might get detention.

Our opinions

We have managed to find some things we like about schools fifty years ago and some things we like about schools today. We like that in 1967 they didn't wear uniforms but we don't like corporal punishment. What we liked about schools in 2017 is you get a choice of what you want to eat. You also don't have to eat everything. You can use white boards.

Albena-"I would prefer to go to school in 2017 because you get a choice of what you want to eat."

Alfie-"I like to go to school in 2017 because you don't get hit with a cane."

Albena Nenova and Alfie Ambridge

Comparing School Life in 1967 and Today

School Life in 1967

In 1967 school life was quite different. The curriculum was different because the teachers taught whatever they wanted to teach. They never went to the Headteacher and asked what they should teach. Mostly, children watched TV to learn or spent the year writing in a booklet. For lunches, dinner ladies just put whatever horrible, disgusting, revolting food they had on children's plates. Children had to eat whatever there was on their pates, before they went out to play. Some schools had dinner ladies to stand at each table and make sure everybody had eaten everything. Other schools had table leaders who had to eat everybody's leftovers. In class there were black boards and desks were arranged in rows. Sometimes, head teachers had a cane and if you were naughty you would get whacked. Some teachers kept a ruler in class in case anyone was naughty. Sometimes you would get hit around the ear.

School Life in 2017

Although some things are the same, many aspects of school life have changed in 2017. The Curriculum has changed because the government does not let you teach whatever you want to teach. The teachers plan your lessons. Every year group across the country learns the same things. The school's lunches are different because children are encouraged to eat nice, delicious, healthy food - we don't get forced to eat everything on our plates. We now have choices between home packed lunch, hot meals, vegetarian meals and sometimes school packed lunches, but only in the summer! In modern classrooms, we have tables instead of desks and children don't store their supplies in the tables. We now have lockers and trays to put our work in. We also have an interactive white board, so the teachers don't have to get covered in white, dusty chalk. No one has corporal punishments anymore, you just get shouted at if you are really bad. You might also have to go along the corridor and talk to the headteacher or miss break times.

Our Opinions

We have managed to find some things we like about schools 50 years ago and some things we like about school today. We think that 1967 schools were good because you could have a class pet. We like that you could watch TV to learn because we don't do that now and it would be quicker, better and it's fun! We think that schools in 2017 are good because we get to have discos and school trips quite often. We also like to use technology with our work because it is fun!

Maisey- "I would prefer to go to school in 2017, because you can have a packed lunch and there are now better things to use in school (eg. Whiteboards, books and stationery)"
Jasmin-"I would prefer to go to school in 2017, because I wouldn't get whacked with a cane."

Maisey Bell and Jasmin Fisher

Comparing School Life in 1967 and Today

School life in 1967

In 1967 school life was quite different. They did not have a curriculum because the government did not tell them what to teach, so the teachers made it up as they went along! Often they would put a TV or radio on to learn. In class the pupils sat at desks facing the front in cramped lines. They wrote on blackboards with chalk! Also their desks lifted up and inside was a space where there books and pencil cases could be kept. Some classes also had a class pet. Unfortunately school lunches were often horrible and disgusting. They didn't get a choice unless they were allergic to the food and weren't allowed to leave the table until they had finished all there food. Corporal punishment was used when someone was naughty. If they were naughty they would get hit by a cane, belt, rubber or a shoe.

School life in 2017

Although some things are the same, many aspects of school life have changed in 2017. Nowadays we do have a curriculum where the government tells the teachers what to teach. In the morning we have to do English and Maths. In class the equipment is quite different. One of the things that has changed are the blackboards, the teachers now use whiteboards and interactive boards which connect to the teacher's laptop. Also, the class tables have changed. The desks are in tables of six and they do not have a space inside, instead we have pots, trays and lockers for storage. The lunches are different because we can chose between different choices. We are not forced to eat all our lunch. We do not have corporal punishment instead we have a zone board. We do not get hit with a hard, wooden ruler.

Our opinions

We have managed to find to find some things we like about schools fifty years ago and some things we like about schools today. What we like about 1967 is that they had a class pet so they could look at it during class. Also they did have school uniform but they did not have to wear it. What we like about 2017, is not having corporal punishment because we think it is not nice. We also like that we can choose our lunches.

Lila - "I would prefer to go to school in 2017 because the teacher helps you when you need help in class."

Jayley - "I would prefer to go to school in 2017 because we get educated well."

Jayley Thompson and Lila Bellamy

Comparing School Life in 1967 and Today

School Life in 1967

In 1967, school life was quite different. Children were forced to have school dinners and they were also forced to eat everything even if they didn't like it but they didn't have to eat it if they were allergic to the food. In some schools, a child had to eat all the leftovers from their table. The classrooms were laid out very differently than they are today. The classrooms had blackboards that you wrote on with chalk. Tables were set up in rows facing the front and they had lift up desks to store belongings in. They also used to have class pets in some classes. The equipment they used to have in classrooms were radios and T.Vs. In 1967, corporal punishment was allowed. Good children had nothing to worry about but naughty children got hit, had rubbers thrown at them, had wooden rulers whacked on them and sometimes they were caned. The teachers didn't teach their class as much because children mainly learnt from the T.V., radios or textbooks.

School Life in 2017

Although, some things are the same, many aspects of school life have changed in 2017. Now we have a variety of lunch choices. These days, you are not forced to eat everything on your plate. In 2017, class equipment is very different to how it was in 1967. In 2017, we have large, clear interactive white boards with electronic pens. We also have drawers and lockers to store our things in. In 2017, corporal punishment isn't allowed. These days you stay in at break time, get sent to the headteacher's office or get moved down the zone board. In 2017, teachers plan what they are going to teach their class and every year 6 class all have to learn the same thing. In some schools at the start and end of some curriculum projects children have a fun day. Instead of listening to radios and watching T.V all day teachers actually teach you something.

Our Opinions

We have managed to find some things we like about schools fifty years ago and some things we like about schools today. The first thing we like about school life in 1967, is that they had a school pet (rabbits, guinea pigs, hamsters, fish or budgie). We also like that they had lift up desks to store stuff in and corporal punishment. We don't agree its right to hit children but it creates a lot of discipline. Finally we like that you don't have to wear school uniform because you were free to wear whatever you like but it wasn't fair to less fortunate children. What we like about schools today is that we have air conditioning and central heating. Finally, teachers help you if you're stuck.

Charlie- "I would prefer to go to school in 2017 because teachers are much nicer to pupils."

Mia Rose- "I would prefer to go to school in 1967 because there is more discipline."

Mia Rose Boswell and Charlie Hammond

Comparing School life in 1967 and Today

School life in 1967

In 1967 school life was quite different. In the classrooms in 1967 the children sat in rows of two's facing the front, it was very cramped. They had lots of different equipment like a blackboard and sometimes a class pet. Children's lunches were usually terrible and you had to eat all the food on your plate unless you were a vegetarian or allergic. At most schools the horrible cook would dump disgusting food on the pupil's plate and you didn't get a choice. You had many different punishments! One of the punishment was getting hit with a cane by the head teacher but that was only used when you had done something really bad. The class teachers made you write lines or threw board rubbers at the pupils. Finally, the teachers may smack you on the hand with a ruler. Instead of the teachers having a particular thing to teach they could teach anything they wanted to. The teacher didn't always teach the pupils they either listened to the radio or watched TV to teach the pupils.

School life in 2017

Although some things are the same, many aspects of school life have changed in 2017. In the classrooms now the desks are in tables of six. The equipment now is very different to now, whiteboards are used instead of black boards. The lunches in 2017 are very yummy and you don't have to eat it all. Now, you can get a big range of choices to eat but in 1967 you had barely any choice. Nowadays, sadly teachers are not allowed to hit you when you are naughty. The punishments now are missing your break or lunch and you go to the head teacher's office. We have a zone board with warnings but when you get to red there is a bigger punishment. But if you are good you get a reward. Nowadays you have a curriculum that is given to the teachers which tells them what they have to teach. As you can now tell school life is now very different.

Our opinions

We have managed to find things we like about school life fifty years ago and things we like about school life today. We like that in 1967 they had school pets and that pupils could choose what they would like to wear. We also like that they sat in rows of twos and they listened to the radio and watched TV to learn. Although we like things about 1967 we also like things about 2017. Firstly, we like that the cooks are very friendly and they serve good food. The school's white boards are electronic (interactive whiteboards) we also like that you have a curriculum to learn in each year.

Annabella-"I would prefer going to school in 2017 because I like having iPads and electronics. Also I like the pool because it has heating and changing rooms."

Ruby –"I would prefer to go to school in 2017 because you get tastier food than in 1967 and it has central heating in the classrooms for when it is cold, and air conditioning for when it is hot."

Annabella Johnson and Ruby Stevens

Comparing School life in 1967 and Today

School life in 1967

In 1967 school was quite different. In class they had blackboards instead of whiteboards. Also, they sat in long, straight rows facing the front. They had desks that they could lift up and put their belongings in. Sometimes they had a class pet. Also, the lunches weren't always good but if you went to a good school with a good cook then they might taste nice. You had to eat all your food even if you didn't like it. The teachers didn't have a curriculum so they could teach whatever they wanted. Despite that, they normally watched TV and listened to the radio. If you were naughty you would be hit by the slipper, belt, ruler or blackboard rubber but if you were really naughty you would be sent to the headmaster to get the cane.

School life today

Although some things are the same, many aspects of school life has changed in 2017. Nowadays, the class equipment is different we have interactive whiteboards as well as whiteboards. Now we sit in tables of six and only move them for tests. The lunches are also different. Today, we can chose what we want to eat (hot, cold, vegetarian and packed lunch) now we don't have to eat everything. All the teachers in a year have to teach the same thing. Luckily corporal punishment is no longer so no more cane. You would be put on a warning, yellow and worst of all red and then you'll miss break.

Our opinions

We have managed to find out some things we like about schools 50 years ago and schools today. We like that corporal is no longer. Also we think that having a class pet would be nice. Also, we think that watching TV or listening to the radio but not always and we wouldn't want to have lunches in 1967.

Ella – "I would prefer to go to school in 2017 because I don't like the idea of corporal punishment and I don't think the children should have to eat all their lunch."

Daniel – "I would prefer to go to school in 2017 because I like the idea of ipads."

Daniel Hilton and Ella Hughes

Comparing School Life in 1967 and Today

School Life in 1967

In 1967, school life was quite different. Back then, they had corporal punishment. If the children were naughty they would go to their Headmaster's office and get hit by a hard, brown cane. If they were bad in class they would get hit by a ruler or made to do lines. The lunches were also different. Sometimes the lunches were horrible and disgusting. If you didn't eat all your food you wouldn't be allowed to go out and play. They only had one choice of food to eat. They also had a different layout in their classroom. They had desks that faced the front and they were lift up desks so they could put some of their belongings in it. They didn't have many male teachers or any teaching assistants but teachers could teach whatever they wanted. The teachers didn't tell the children how to do the lessons, often pupils were meant to follow instructions in textbooks.

School Life in 2017

Although some things are the same, many aspects of school life have changed in 2017. Today the teachers aren't allowed to use horrible, violent corporal punishment. Also, at lunch we don't have to eat all our lunch and we have more than one choice. Now we have different equipment like the desks, rulers, white boards, interactive white boards and more modern electronics. The layout has also changed because we don't have desks, we have tables of six children. The curriculum has changed because the teachers have to teach what the government tell them to teach. In 1967 they didn't have homework in primary schools very often and now we have lots! In the playground we have bigger climbing equipment and bigger fields. We also play different games in the playground.

Our Opinion

We have managed to find some things we like about schools 50 years ago and some things we like about schools today. In 2017, we like the school dinners. In 1967, we like corporal punishment because it gives children a lesson not to be naughty. We like in 1967 that you have to eat everything on your plate to go out because it means you won't be fussy.

Leia: "I like both because I like corporal punishment in 1967 but I like school dinner in 2017"

Tillie: "I would prefer to go to school in 2017 because for school dinners you get to pick a choice of food to eat."

Leia Stewart and Tillie Farrell

Comparing school life in 1967 and Today

School Life in 1967

In 1967, school life was quite different. Firstly, teachers were allowed to teach the children whatever they wanted. Secondly, teachers didn't do much teaching because they had a radio or TV programme and the children would watch or listen to learn. Thirdly, school lunches in 1967 were quite different to now. The children had to eat all of their dinner otherwise they wouldn't be able to go outside! In the classroom the desks were set out in rows that were tightly packed together. Also, the desks were able to pull-up. In addition to this, they used a blackboard and they used white, smooth chalk to write with. Also, many classes had a class pet that one person would take home at the end of a week. Schools also used corporal punishment. They had a punishment of getting hit with a ruler or if the children did something really naughty they would have to go to the headmaster's office to get hit with his hurtful, stinging cane.

School life in 2017

Although some things are the same, many aspects of school life have changed in 2017. In most schools the classes have spread out tables instead of tightly packed desks. Now we have interactive whiteboards and computers to type, draw and write on. Also, in 2017 we have a different system for corporal punishment. Many schools use warnings from teachers instead of getting told off straight away. Often now in school you have to stay in during your break time or lunch time to do your homework. If you're good you get a prize or sweet maybe once a week. Also, at lunch time you don't have to eat all of your lunch. There are dinner choices and you can have a school packed lunch and home packed lunch.

Our Opinions

We have managed to find some things we like about school fifty years ago and some things we like about schools today. One thing we like about schools fifty years ago is that they had a class pet in the classroom. Now, we like that we don't use mean, hurtful corporal punishment. Also we don't get hit by a ruler or a cane! We like school now because we can use the computers which gives us ideas for our work. We like school in 1967 because you could wear whatever you wanted and you could wear something different every day. Also, we like school in 2017 because we get to go on exciting school trips.

Alf- "I would prefer to go to school in 2017 because I would rather choose out of a couple of dinner choices and have an option to have a pack lunch."

Clarice- "I would prefer to go to school in 2017 because I won't get hit from the head teacher's cane."

Alf Wells and Clarice Messenger

Comparing School Life in 1967 and Today

School Life in 1967

In 1967 school life was quite different. School desks were in long, straight rows facing the front. The desks were quite packed together. Unlike today, many classrooms had a school pet, usually a hamster, rabbit, fish or bird. Most classrooms had a rolling black board to get a new writing surface. The teachers used chalk to write on the board. There was usually a radio on the wall and a TV somewhere in the classroom. Schools didn't have teaching assistants. Curriculum was different in 1967, teachers could teach whatever they wanted to teach. You would get taught by a TV or a radio. The food the cooks gave you was only sometimes tasty. The food was served in pots. You didn't have a choice about what to eat. You were not allowed to go onto the playground until you had eaten every last bit of food on your plate. In addition to this, some schools had someone on each table to eat the leftovers of other peoples' meals. Corporal punishments included caning by the headmaster and being beaten by the teacher. Also, you could be whacked with a ruler. If you were really naughty you could be caned with a wooden pole.

School Life in 2017

Although some things are the same, many aspects of school life has changed in 2017. Class equipment and layout was different in 1967, but now the desks are more spread out. Also, desks are put together to make a table. In 2017 there are interactive white boards and computers. Teachers use white boards and rubbers instead of blackboards. Nowadays, there is a curriculum that all schools have to follow. Teachers do the teaching instead of working through a book. Lunches are much nicer in 2017. You get to have a choice, you can have: hot meal, roll, vegetarian or you could bring in your own lunch. You don't have to eat all your lunch. In 2017 corporal punishment is illegal. Instead you are told off, moved down the zone board, given detention or even expelled or suspended. Rarely, schools went on trips in 1967, now in 2017 schools go on fun, adventure packed trips.

Our Opinions

We have managed to find some things we like about schools fifty years ago and some things we like about schools today. One thing, we like about schools in 1967 is you got to wear whatever you like because we have lots of nice things to wear at home. In 2017 we like that you have choices at lunch and electronic gadgets to help us with our learning.

Hollie-"I would prefer to go to school in 1967 because you have lift up desks and you learnt from TV and radios'. Also, I think that corporal punishment is a good idea to make children respect the teacher."

Jaidan- "I would prefer to go to school in 1967 because you get to see the school pet and teachers get to teach whatever they wanted.

Hollie King and Jaidan Childs

Comparing School Life in 1967 and Today

School Life in 1967

In 1967 school life was quite different. In the classroom they sat in tight, pushed together rows at the back of the room. Teachers used blackboards and sometimes when they'd finished with one side you'd pull it down for a new one. The teachers could teach pupils whatever they wanted. The children needed to call their male teachers Sir. Everyone listened to the radio each morning and had a book with hymns and songs to sing along to. They had to eat everything, even if they didn't like it, before they could leave. The cook's silver, metal, hot pots had lots of mushy, disgusting food inside. Unfortunately, if you were bad you would be sent to the headmaster's and slapped with something like a cane. If you weren't listening in class you would be hit with a ruler, or sent to the front of the class and whacked on the bum!

School Life in 2017

Although some things are the same, many aspects of school life have changed in 2017. In 2017 children sit in tables of six. Often the teachers have whiteboards or interactive whiteboards. Children use whiteboards to. Nowadays, the government tell the teachers what to teach so everyone learns the same. In 2017 we now get a great, big choice of what we want to eat. Now we can eat as much as we want. Now we still get sent to the head teacher's office if we are naughty, but now instead of getting hit, the head teacher speaks to you about why you have been sent there.

Our Opinions

We have managed to find some things we like about schools fifty years ago and some things we like about schools today. One thing we like about 1967 schools was that they had a class pet. Another thing we like is that the childrens' school uniform was optional and normal clothes are a lot more comfy. The thing we like about schools now are: you get a choice of school dinners because if you don't like one thing you can have another. Also we like that we have tables of six because it's more brains so your work will be better.

Imogen-"I would prefer to go to school in 2017 because there is no corporal punishment and also the teachers teach more themselves so they can explain it better."

Jayden- "I would prefer to go to school in 2017 because you get more choices in school for lunch and you get more equipment to play with."

Jayden Moore and Imogen Wilson

Mr Carr's Class; 4T

From left to right in both pictures.
Top row: Amy-Mae, Harry, Ellie, Mr Carr, Sasha, Evie, Billy
Middle row: Kieran, Sienna, Ciara, Tom, Hayden, Amy, Charlotte, Oscar
Sitting: Olivia, Jessica, Ty, Evan, Freddie, Charlie, Thomas, Orlaith, Violet
Bottom row: Lexi, Olivia, Eva, Tommy, Lily, Freya, April

School life – 1967 and 2017

School life was very different in 1967. The expectations at school, lessons they were taught and attitudes towards education were all very different to today. To start with, children used to walk to school, no matter how far away they lived. Very few families owned cars. One of the main differences were punishments the teachers used. If they misbehaved or did not do their homework, children would be sent to the head mistress. This could sometimes involve being hit with a cane. In addition to this, in PE, some schools had children dressed in underwear and vests. In 1967, the teachers would use blackboards and chalk. Fifty years ago, the desks held children's personal equipment that they would need for the lessons and classrooms were organised in rows. Schools had very mixed expectations on their uniforms. Some schools allowed you to wear your own clothes to school, others did not.

In comparison, a typical school day in 2017 would begin with a bus or car journey to school, although some children still walk to school. Today, the worst punishment or sanction for misbehaviour would be your mum being called by the teacher or an after school detention. Nowadays, we can wear polo tops and shorts or jogging bottoms, in PE, depending on the weather. PE is probably more enjoyable now because you do not have to wear your underwear and vests. Fifty years later, we have interactive whiteboards and technology plays a more important role in the classroom. In today's society, we have tables, not sitting in rows, to encourage collaborative learning. In 2017, nearly all schools wear uniforms.

We would rather go to school in 1967 because they did not have technology which can be easily misused. Lessons relied more on books than technology, which means the facts inside are normally more truthful and therefore they learnt more. We also like the idea of having a desk where we can store all of our belongings, such as our pencil cases.

Olivia Gibbins and Sasha Swindale

School Life from 1967 to 2017

Fifty years ago, school life was very different to today. First of all, there were no pre-schools or nurseries, whereas fifty years later, there are. That meant, when going to school, it would be the first time children would be away from home without their parents. Another difference is girls and boys went to separate schools but today, girls and boys go to the same school, sometimes separate. St Mary's itself began as separate schools for the boys, girls and infants. As some schools had no uniform, pupils could wear what they wanted, however jeans, referred to as dungarees at the time, were strictly forbidden. Unfortunately, school dinners were not that nice so some pupils went home for lunch, though today people have schools dinners or bring a packed lunch to school. A typical school dinner may have consisted of lumpy mashed potato. The lessons depended on what the teacher wanted to teach, so it could have been maths all day... oh no!

A school day in 2017 normally starts with children walking to school, getting a train or bus or going by car. In the past, people would have had to walk to school, however near or far they were. Whereas in 2017, we use interactive whiteboards, laptops and iPads, comparatively, in 1967, a blackboard and chalk was used. Another comparison, is in 1967, a nit nurse and the school dentist came regularly, and hearing and eye tests were taken at school. This however rarely happens in 2017, though in year 6, weights and heights of children are taken. In the past, girls would have had to wear hats with elastic during lunch. Today, every school has a uniform, although some are stricter than others.

In our opinion, we would have rather have gone to school in 2017. One of the main reasons is in 1967 P.E would have been done in pants and vest or knickers and vest, in all weather, whereas today, we have polos and shorts. On the other hand, school in 1967 does seem appealing because there was no uniform. We also think it would be quite cool if there were desks with lids that lifted up. In 2017, we have tables with everything on top. We preferred school dinners in 2017 because in 1967, they were almost inedible. The last reason why we would not have wanted to go to school in 1967 is the pupils were forced to drink watery, lukewarm milk.

Ellie Cook and Lily Stanbridge

1967 vs 2017 – school life

School was very different in 1967. Did you know, that they did not have a curriculum? In comparison to today, when the national curriculum dictates what teachers must teach, schools in 1967 were far more teacher dependent. Classes would complete lessons, based on what the teacher wanted to teach. One of the main differences was that in P.E they wore their pants or knick-nocks with a vest, even in rainy, stormy weather, whereas we wear black shorts and coloured polo shirts with trainers. The actual lessons taught in PE were also different, with many 60s lessons involving cross country or gymnastics, sometimes on the playground. In today`s society, our desks are put together into a table of six so we can work collaboratively, which means we work together. Their desks were in pairs and tight together, with each desk storing the child's personal belongings inside its lid.

The structure of the school day was also different. At lunch times, mothers would stay at home so their children could come home to have their lunch, if they wanted to. People who were packed lunches nowadays would have had to go home to eat and walk back after they had eaten, if they went to school in 1967. They drunk daily milk. School dinners would stay at school. Generally, in 1967, when pupils misbehaved they got hit with a cane on their palms and buttocks for their punishment. They would commonly be whipped with a ruler or a cane. In comparison, if children misbehaved today, they have to stay in class for break time or after school detention. Pupils would have to walk to school even if they were miles and miles away from the school. Fifty years later, we can travel to school by using trains, buses, cars and bikes.

In our opinion, we would prefer to go to school in 2017 because there`s a variety of technology such as computers and iPads. These help us learn and make our lessons more fun. We also have a curriculum so we are doing what was planned and this helps us build our learning year after year.

Eva Keen and Evie Segust

School life in 1967 and 2017

School was very different in 1967. One of the main differences was that children had to wear their pants/knickers and vests for PE, regardless of the weather. Although technology plays a major part in classrooms today, in 1967 they had blackboards, not whiteboards, and did not use computers and iPads. In 1967, the cane was often used for punishments and, depending on the misbehaviour, they might have been hit more than once. The layout and structure of the classrooms was also different. In lessons, children would share desks and store all their belongings inside them. Though not all schools had a uniform, schools that did were very strict. An example of the rules was that boys had to have short hair.

Fifty years later, in 2017, schools are very different. For example, today we wear a PE kit in our lessons. Nowadays, we have whiteboards to write on and an interactive whiteboard at the front of the classroom. In schools today, if we have been naughty, we miss break times and lunchtimes. We also sometimes have after school detentions but nothing as scary as the cane! In modern times, we share tables so we can work together. Also, today our hair style does not matter but girls have to tie it up for PE.

We would want to go to school in 2017 because if you lived a mile away in 1967 you would still have to walk and today we do not have to walk to school all the time. Another reason is that you do not get hit with a cane for a punishment. We also like our school dinners because they are nice and have a wide range of choice, unlike in 1967.

Oscar Milroy and Hayden Boldick

School life – 1967 to 2017

School was very different in 1967. Schools in the sixties were different because they would have desks, which the children could store their things in. Also, they would be working individually or mostly in pairs. One of the main differences was that if children were naughty they would have got sent to the Head Mistress. While they were there, they would have got hit by a cane. Depending on how naughty they were, they could have got hit more than once. In 1967, they had no nursery or pre-school when they were little. At different schools, some of them gave homework out every day and some of the schools gave no homework at all. St Mary's ex-pupils have said they received homework once a week. In 1967, the school dinners were not great. At some schools, they did not have real vegetarian options.

There were differences in the lessons taught and how they were taught. In PE, for example, they wore vests with knickers and pants but in 2017 we wear a PE kit with either plimsolls or trainers. Fifty years later, most years get Maths and English homework, including spellings, times tables and reading. In the 60s, they had blackboards with chalk, unlike in 2017, where we have whiteboards with whiteboard pens and an interactive board. Also in 1967, they had to have their hair similar to everyone else's but in 2017 there is more freedom over choice of hairstyle.

We would want to go to school in 2017 because you did not have to do the same lesson every day. Another reason is that we think school dinners were not great and comparatively, school dinners in 2017 are better because we have a vegetarian option and there is more choice over food.

Harry Brant and Ty Butler

School life in 1967 to 2017

A typical school day in 1967 would begin with walking to school, regardless of where you lived. When at school, the teacher would begin with counting the pupils and collecting the school dinner money. Then they would start lessons with whatever the teacher wanted to teach because there was no national curriculum. This meant that there was no standard teaching for children nationwide and topics and subjects varied between schools. A P.E kit was not used and instead they would have to do it in their pants or knickers and vest, whatever the weather. For other lessons, they would use a black board and chalk and sit in rows, not tables like today.
When a child was naughty, they would be punished with either the dunce hat or the cane. School dinners in 1967 were not as pleasant as those eaten today as they did not have a choice of what they would have unlike today.

    Comparatively, a typical school day in 2017 would begin with either walking, driving or catching the bus or train to school. Then the teacher would call the register and start with either English or maths, followed by lessons such as history and computing. A government agreed national curriculum is used by the majority of schools to ensure of the same age are taught the same topics and subjects nationwide. If they were doing P.E, children would wear coloured polo tops and shorts or jogging bottoms if it was cold. In 2017, technology is used a lot in lessons, including iPads, laptops, computers and an interactive white board. For punishments, children would miss their break time or lunchtime and sometimes miss time after school if they got a detention. In 2017, the school dinners offer a wider choice of foods and some people bring their own packed lunch from home.

    In our opinion, we would prefer to go to school in 2017 because in lessons we use electronics to make things easier, for example you can use laptops to type things up instead of writing which will be slower. Another reason for this is that we have a variety of lessons each day so we learn the things that are important. Our final reason is in 2017, although we both have packed lunches, we think the school dinners are better.

Evan Wonfor and Jessica Mitchell

School life in 1967 and 2017

School was very different in 1967. One of the main differences was they had to wear knickers/pants and a vest for PE. Another difference is they used a cane for punishment. They also used blackboards with chalk, instead of whiteboards. The classrooms were organised so the children sat in rows. The desks held equipment for the lesson. They had to walk to school every day, no matter how far away they lived. In 1967 the school lunches were not great and the choice of food was very limited. In some schools, they prayed before they ate and before they went back to their classrooms.

School life is not the same in 2017. Nowadays, in PE we wear jogging bottoms if it's cold and shorts if it's warm. Some schools wear PE tops, which shows which house colour they are in. In 2017, we do not always have to walk to school because more people can afford cars. Lunches in 2017 have more options than in 1967 and we also have vegetarian options. We do not have to use a cane for punishment but the punishments can include having an after school for a detention. At school today we use mini whiteboards and a big whiteboard for the teacher to write on. We have computers and the teachers use an interactive whiteboard. Comparatively, we sit in tables so we can work together.

In our opinion, we would have preferred to go to school in 2017 because the food is nicer, rather than lumpy mash, we have pizza. We get to wear PE clothes. Unlike in 1967, our PE lessons take place inside if it is raining. We now wear school uniform so it shows we are a school together.

Olivia Frisch and Ciara Scripps

School life - 1967 to 2017

School was very different in 1967. One of the main differences was that not all schools wore school uniform. Also, if you were naughty you could get hit with a cane or a slipper. Children sat at desks, which were in rows not in groups or tables. They also sat in pairs and stored their equipment and belongings in their desks. There were no computers and whiteboards, you would use a blackboard and chalk. They did PE in their pants and vests. Also, everybody walked to school no matter how far away they lived. Teachers taught the lessons however they wanted to, as there was no national curriculum. Lunches were often not very tasty and teachers ate in the dining hall with the children. At St Mary's in 1967, they did four lessons before lunch and four lessons after lunch. Normally, Maths and English would be doubled. Fifty years ago, they played football and climbed on the climbing frame at lunch times.

In 2017, everyone wears school uniform. Nowadays, a punishment can mean staying in a break time or a lunchtime or having an after school detention. Technology including iPads, computers and interactive whiteboards is used in lessons to help us learn. In the modern day, if you live far away you would probably get a lift from your parents. The government now decide what the teachers have to teach by using the National Curriculum. Fifty years later school, dinners are very delicious and staff would normally eat their lunch in the staff room and the children eat in the dining hall. We do all different topics and the teachers are very friendly and always help you if you need it. We have more homework than people did in 1967.

Our opinion is that we would rather go to school in 1967. Our main reason for this is that we would not have to wear school uniform. Additionally, we like the idea of desks in rows and you can store things in your desks. Also there were no preschools or nurseries so you would not have to start school until the age of five. However, a disadvantage is that you could get hit with a cane or a slipper. And also the swimming pool at St Mary's was not heated!

Billy Pateman and Freddie Arbon

School life-1967 to 2017

A typical day in 1967 would start off with a walk to school, wherever you lived. When the pupils got into class, the teacher would count them all, instead of doing a register. As there was no National Curriculum, the teacher could choose what lesson they taught, when and for how long. Did you know in P.E in 1967 you only wore pants/knickers and a vest, in all weathers? Fifty years ago, if a pupil misbehaved, they would have been beaten with a cane. In some universities and schools, you were not allowed to attend if you did not have the right hair style. School life in 1967 was very different from 2017.

In today's society, every teacher across the country has to teach the same subjects and topics, according to the National Curriculum. For example, in year four we all learn about the Greeks. Nowadays, we have a P.E kit, unlike in 1967, and we wear trainers mainly, not plimsolls. In 2017, we use traffic lights to monitor our behaviour. Although we have a school uniform, there is more freedom over the hairstyles we wish to have. In 2017, we have iPads, laptops and interactive whiteboards, but in 1967 they did not have any of that technology.

We would prefer to go to school in 2017. This is because of the iPads, laptops and other technology, which makes lessons more fun and helps our learning. Also, in P.E, we would not just like to wear our underwear. Another reason for our choice is the dinners now are a lot nicer and pupils can bring their own packed lunches. Also, in the summer, we can go swimming during PE and our pool is heated, unlike it was when the school's pool opened in 1971.

Tom Barnes and Kieran Cody

School life in 1967 and 2017

Schools back in 1967 were very different from today because when you were naughty at school, in 1967, you would be hit with a cane. The curriculum was very different from today. One of the school lessons was PE but you would have to do it in your pants and vest. In comparison to modern schools, school life in 1967 was very strict about uniform. Students were not allowed sleeveless tops or dresses in schools. Boys were not allowed their hair touching their collars and their hair had to be groomed properly. Their desks were open and closable at all times and they could also hold their belongings inside, such as their pencil cases and rubbers. Their tables were always in rows. Back in 1967, their school dinners were not particularly nice for vegetarians but some children would go home for lunch, have their lunch and then they would have to come back to school.

A typical day at school in 2017 starts with either Maths or English. In some schools now, they have equipment all around the room and you have lockers and drawers, instead of open and closable desks. Nowadays, boys and girls are allowed to wear trousers, skirts and shorts. If you are naughty today, you would have to stay in at lunch and break times outside the head mistress or master's office. Today, school dinners involve a wider range of choice and taste better. The student's hair is allowed to be below their shoulders and, in PE, we have house colours and matching t-shirts. We also have the luxury of heated and air conditioned classrooms, which St Mary's did not have in 1967. The pool was not heated either!

We would prefer 2017 school life because in 1967 they had harsher reports at school and the teachers were stricter. Additionally, they had very unpleasant meals that were not as tasty as the ones nowadays.

Charlotte Bridgeman and Violet St John Clarke

School life – 1967 compared to 2017

School life in 1967 was very different to our school life in 2017. There is a difference in the lessons teachers taught and how they taught them. One of the main differences is that they did PE in their knickers/pants and vests. Unlike now, where we wear coloured polo shirts and shorts. Back in the 1960s, they had a blackboard and chalk, whereas now where we have interactive boards and whiteboards. Nowadays, we also have electronic devices, such as iPads and laptops, used in our lessons. Fifty years ago, they had no national curriculum, which meant they would be taught any lesson the teacher wanted to do but now we have a programme of study in schools which is followed nationwide.

There are also major differences in how the classrooms were organised and the structure of the school day. Nowadays, the desks are put together to encourage collaborative learning. Every day, when they had school dinner, the children had to bring money into their teacher. Fifty years ago, they were forced to eat their school dinners even though some of them were awful. Back in 1967, their punishment for misbehaving was they would sit in the corner and have a hat on that said 'D,' which meant dunce which means everyone could see you misbehaved. Also, you would be hit with a cane. At lunch, the teachers would sit on a table in the dining hall and the children would sit away from them.

We would prefer to go to school in 2017 because we would not like to be hit with a cane. Another reason is nowadays we have technology used in our classrooms so we can find information quicker and easier and this helps our learning. The last reason is because we do have fairly good school dinners and no lumpy potatoes!

Amy-Mae Haldenby and Thomas Stonebrook

School life – 1967 to 2017

School life was very different in 1967. One of the main reasons was because they did not have to wear the same uniform. They usually had to do P.E in knickers or pants and a vest. In 1967, the desks stored the children's books and the children's places were squashed together, usually in rows. The desks had a flap on the top and under the flap the children stored all their belongings. Additionally, they had to walk to school, regardless of how far away they lived. As a punishment for bad behaviour, their teachers had a cane to hit the pupils with, normally on the hand or bottom. Fifty years ago, you would have had grades instead of reports. Teachers were much harsher when writing these. In 1967, you were forced to eat at lunch and the teachers sat on a different table from the children. The teachers did not eat in the staff room.

    Nowadays, school life is different. One reason is because we wear the same uniform. In modern society, for P.E, we wear a t-shirt and shorts or jogging bottoms, if it is cold. We can now choose if we walk to school. Today the teachers do not use a cane (thankfully!). The worst punishment you could get would be an after school detention or the teachers calling your mum. Also, we now have tables to work collaboratively, instead of sitting at individual desks. Our tables do not store our books in, we have lockers instead. In 2017, we are not forced to eat. At lunchtimes, the teachers eat in the staff room and not the dining hall.

    In our opinion we would prefer to go to school in 2017, instead of 1967. Two reasons are because you do not have to walk to school because some people live far away. Also, we would not like to do P.E in knickers or pants and a vest. Additionally, we would not like to get hit by a cane and be forced to eat, which did happen in 1967. Another reason is because we would not like to use wooden balls and bats for P.E because it could be dangerous.

Freya Lovett and Sienna Salmons

School life 1967 and 2017

Going to school was very different in 1967, when this St Mary's building opened. In 1967, the students would have to usually wear vests and pants for P.E, no matter what the weather was like. Teachers taught whatever lesson they wanted to teach that day. Also, another difference is that fifty years ago, they did not have nursery or pre-school places for children. In addition to this, you would also have to walk to school, even if you lived far away because not many people owned cars and most did not drive anyway.

   Nowadays we have a P.E. kit designed for schools, which usually is a polo top and shorts or, if it's cold, you would wear jogging bottoms and you could do P.E inside. Schools today do not have as much freedom as fifty years ago because a National Curriculum is set for teachers. Although in modern times, we have pre-schools and nurseries so that children can be schooled from 2-4 years of age, they did not have these in 1967. Additionally, in 2017, if you live far from school, you can catch a bus or a train or get a lift from your parents.

   We would rather go to school in 2017 because you can start school at a younger age as in 1967 you would not have nurseries or pre-schools. This would help you learn more. Another reason, is that nowadays pupils are warmer in P.E. and fifty years ago you would freeze if the weather was bad. In modern times, we are lucky enough to not always have to walk to school.

Lexi Baker and Amy O'Reilly

School life -1967 to 2017

Compared to today, school life was very different in 1967. One of the main differences is the lessons teachers taught, how they taught them, including punishments for misbehaviour, and for how long they taught the lessons. One major differences was PE. You had to wear your underpants and vest in all weathers, inside and out but now you have to wear a polo shirt with tracksuit bottoms or shorts. Teachers also had a choice about what subjects they wanted to teach, while today the government use a National Curriculum to make sure all teachers are teaching the same objectives to children of the same ages. In 1967, if pupils misbehaved, they got hit with a cane whereas now you would get a detention.

    Most people's opinions on school dinners from 1967 were that they were not very nice but now they are generally much better. There is also a wider range of foods and a vegetarian option for those having school dinners. Back in 1967, some people went home for lunch as most mothers did not work in 1967. Sometimes, the dinner monitors made you eat all of you lunch even if it made you sick, which happened sometimes! If you went to school in 1967, you would have to walk, no matter how far away you lived. In modern society, we have cars and buses for that. Sometimes, you could not get into certain schools because you did not have the right hairstyle but now you can have your hair in a lot more hairstyles. Some schools are however stricter about school uniforms nowadays, in comparison to those in 1967.

    In conclusion, we would prefer to go to school in 2017 because you do not get hit with the cane and the food is much nicer. We also think this because we do not want to do PE in our underwear. There are also major differences to St Mary's that mean we would prefer to go to school in 2017, such as the air conditioning, heating and heated swimming pool.

April Henshaw and Tommy Martin

School life in 1967 vs 2017

Back in 1967, school was very different. One of the main differences was you had to wear knickers/pants and vest in PE. Another difference was you could have got punished by getting hit with a cane, slipper or ruler. Each day the pupils would have their daily milk. In 1967, some school dinners were not great, they ate off china plates, which you had to be careful of because if you dropped them they could easily smash. In school, they had black boards and chalk. If the teacher wanted to do a certain subject all day, they did that. Back then they had a school nurse. When it was raining, at break or lunchtimes, they had no entertainment or games so they would they had to entertain themselves by talking to each other. You had text books to copy out of instead of challenges to choose your task from.

In modern times, we have a curriculum that means the teachers have to teach certain subjects. Technology plays a big part in lessons with iPads, laptops and interactive white boards. School dinners are much nicer in 2017. There is a wider choice of foods available, including a vegetarian option. For PE, we wear coloured polo shirts with shorts or tracksuit bottoms. You do not have to drink your daily milk. For punishment, you do not get hit with a cane. Punishments nowadays could involve having to miss your break or lunchtime.

We would rather go to school in 2017 because school dinners are much nicer. Also, you do not get hit with a cane and you do not have to do PE in your vest and underwear. We also have better technology, better equipment and teachers. The classrooms help you more with your learning and lessons seem more exciting than in 1967.

Charlie Andrew and Orlaith Kinloch

Year 5

'Popular culture of the 1960s'

Year 5 children have written historical reports about a variety of themes that help to capture the culture of the 1960s. Children have researched a wide range of areas including; family life, television, radio, fashion, music and art. For some of you we hope this has brought back some nostalgic moments!

Miss Charlwood's Class; 5C

From left to right in both pictures.
Top row: Miss Charwood, Ellie, Josh, Rebecca, Eliza, Nicholas, Nancy, Matilda, Mae, Jake, Mr Faint
Middle row: Anna-Lilja, Benjamin, George, Lucy, Evan, Megan, Arthur, Harry, Rebecca
Sitting: Jack, Poppy, Ruby, Ellie, Jesse, Martin, Lennie, Amy, Macie, Saranya, Isabel

1960s Lucky Leisure

Introduction

The 1960s was a decade of change when people had more opportunities for leisure and entertainment activities. People had more disposable income so they could spend it on clothing, music and holidays. Teens had their own likes and dislikes. This report will look at what families, teenagers, and children did in their leisure time.

Families

Leisure in the 1960s changed most for families because adults had well paid jobs so they had more money to spend on fun activities and holidays. Families started going on package foreign holidays mainly in Spain because it was not too far. Coloured TVs were introduced to the UK so more families watched television. The number of restaurants increased so a wider range of food was introduced so families went out to eat with greater frequency. More and more motorways were created so families could not only go on foreign holidays, but also holidays in Britain.

Teenagers

Teenagers in the 1960s had a lot more freedom than their parents. This is because they didn't have the restrictions of rationing and war that their parents faced. Teenagers left school at the age of 15 meaning they got a job early in their life so they earned money to spend on records, clothes and other items. Some teens went to music concerts and cinemas. At the cinemas, they mostly played foreign films. The young generation used to carry around transistor radios to listen to their favourite radio stations or songs. They were like the iphone of the 60's.

Children

Children in the 60's liked to play with various toys and do different activities. Children often played a game called Knock Down Ginger. In this game, children would knock at someone's door then run off. Some children bought Airfix kits which were plastic plane models that they could build themselves. On weekends, children sometimes went on scout camps. In 1960, Lego came to Britan and was an instant hit with children because it got them more creative. This is because they could build whatever they wanted (cars, houses, cities etc).

Conclusion

As shown above, there were many changes in 1960's leisure. Most activities people do today are similar to the things people did in the 1960's. For example, teenagers went to concerts and they still do now but in much larger numbers. Technology has changed lots through time which has had a large impact on how people spend their leisure time. Developments in communication have meant that people now have the internet, mobile phones and many more ways to interact. Some people think texting through a screen is a good development and others think differently and prefer it how it was in the 60s.

Nick Frisch and Ellie Bostock

> Radio Caroline was the first pirate radio station in the UK.

> Music played a massive part in 1960 leisure.

60s Terrific TV

The 1960s was a decade of great change. It was during this time when older children had different opinions to their parents especially in the programmes they liked watching. If the 50s were the innocent childhood, then the 60s were the rebellious adolescence of TV. This means that in the 50s TV shows were calm, lovely and sweet, but in the 60s there was more action in the programmes. This text will explain TV in the 1960s.

TV

In the 60s, there were more children's television programmes than ever before, such as 'The Magic Roundabout', 'Basil Brush' and 'Trumpton'. Most people only had a TV in the late 50s and early 60s, so if they didn't have a tv, they went round friend's houses to watch important shows. Lots of bands had TV shows to publicise themselves. There were several breaks between shows, which were hour intervals. Where a cardbord sign was put up in front of the screen saying "please do not adjust your set." It said this as if the person watching did adjust their set, then they would lose the show.

End of broadcasting sign.

and probably not get the channel back in time for the next programme.

Colour

TV in the 1960s became more popular when it changed from black and white to colour. On the 1st July 1967, BBC2 broadcasted the Wimbledons women's singles final in colour. By mid 1968 nearly every programme on BBC2 was in colour. Six months later BBC1 had colour too. By 1969 colour was regularly broadcasted on BBC1 and ITV. Carrying on from 1908 when the first cartoon was created (hand drawn), lots of new cartoons were launched in colour in the 1960s, such as 'Top Cat', 'The Flintstones' and 'Yogi Bear'.

Channels

TV shows were limited in the 1960s as there were only two channels (BBC1 and ITV), until the 1st of April 1964 when BBC2 was launched. This enabled them to spread out the programmes between the channels and

OHHH

MOST WATCHED TELEVISION IN BRITAIN IN THE 1960S

	Title	Channel	Date	Audience (Millions)
1	The World Cup Final 1966 (England vs. Germany)	BBC1	30/07/1966	32.30
2	The Royal Family	BBC1/ITV	21/06/1969	30.69
3	Royal Variety Performance 1965	ITV	14/11/1965	24.20
4	News (John F. Kennedy assassination)	BBC/ITV	22/11/1963	24.15
5	Miss World	BBC1	19/11/1967	23.76
6	Apollo 8 Splashdown	BBC1/ITV	27/12/1968	22.55
7	The London Palladium Show	ITV	03/12/1967	21.89
8	Steptoe and Son	BBC	18/02/1964	21.54
9	Coronation Street	ITV	02/12/1964	21.36
10	Mrs Thursday	ITV	22/03/1966	21.01
11	Secombe and Friends	ITV	13/11/1966	20.79
12	Churchill's Funeral Procession	BBC1/ITV	30/01/1965	20.06
13	Howerd's Hour	ITV	12/05/1968	20.02
14	The Grand National	BBC1	30/03/1968	19.86
15	Market in Honey Lane	ITV	03/04/1967	19.47
16	Double Your Money	ITV	08/11/1966	19.47
17	Take Your Pick	ITV	02/12/1966	19.36
18	The Boat Race	BBC1	30/03/1968	19.36
19	Life With Cooper	ITV	16/03/1968	19.25
20	The Morecambe and Wise Show	ITV	12/11/1967	19.14

launch alot of new popular shows such as 'Coronation street', the news and 'Steptoe and son'. ITV was a commercial channel so it got its money from advertising company's products. However, the BBC channels were paid for by people's licence feas.

This report has explained many things about 1960s television and shows how different it was to today. The main difference between now and the 1960's is that TV shows are available to us 24 hours a day. However, lots of TV shows have survived time or have been relaunched such as 'Blue Peter', 'The Clangers' and 'Sesame street'.

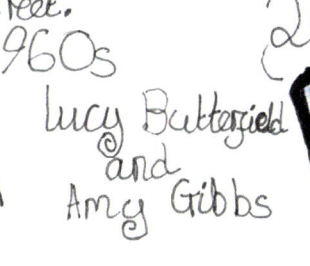

1960s   2017

Lucy Butterfield
and
Amy Gibbs

1960s decade of change

The 1960s was a decade of change, when teenagers could become independent from their parents. In the sixties, teenagers wanted to stand out from society, so they developed their own styles. Different types of music, art and leisure activities at the time, influenced the fashion choices and styles. This report will be focusing on the fashion in the 60s.

Women's fashion

Women's fashion in the 1960s was mainly influenced by the brand new styles of music and bright colours of art. They copied styles from famous models and designers, such as Twiggy and Mary Quant. Because tights had been invented this enabled women to accessorize with shorter skirts. They were eventually renamed mini skirts. People said at the time 'the shorter the skirt the more confident you are.' High neck button up shirts and black turtle neck jumpers were also fashionable, particulary in winter. Shapeless shift dresses featured bright colours and optical art patterns. These were worn to either parties or just for casual home living. Tall (go-go) boots were often worn with slim fit pants, to complete a casual yet stylish look. Ankle boots were often worn on an informal occasion/event and worked well with a pair of bellbottoms. This would create an informal outfit.

Men's fashion

Much like women's fashion, men's fashion evolved through the decade. Men wore banlon shirts that generally required no ironing. They wore tab collar shirts with narrow ties. Older men wore white long sleeved shirts – even lilac. They wore jeans that were tight and had no pleats. Also, they wore pegged pants, which were tight and they wore jeans with rivets and Hush Puppys which were shoes with T-straps, that were suede. They were a brand of shoes. Hush Puppys were worn with bright red socks. Penny loafers were worn for general purposes. Business men wore Wingtips which were smart shoes that were quite often worn for business or sometimes for formal occasions. They were both peforated and serrated round the edges.

Hippies and flower children's fashion

Hippies and flower children wanted to stand out from society because they detested the Vietnam war so, they developed their own clothes and styles. Their clothes were made from natural fibres such as cotten and hemp. They grew their hair very long and wore bandannas. They tie-dyed their clothes by putting elastic bands around them and soaking them in different coloured dyes. Flower children wished for a world of peace and happiness, so they handed out flowers, hence the

the fact they were called flower children. The peace symbol was used to express their disapproval of the Vietnam war. They wore short skirts with suede knee-high boots, in colder weather but on hot summer days they wore sandals. A peasant dress reflected a Renaissance maiden, and flowing ribbons in their hair would enhance the look.

By todays stanards, fashion in the 60s might be classed as 'extreme' or 'over the top'. However, trends in the 60s have massively influenced the items people choose to wear today. For example, mini skirts, hot pants, shift dresses and parkas are still popular choices of clothing throughout the world.

Mae Smith and Matilda Atkins.

OHHH
Fashion in the 1960s

Not only was the 1960s a decade of change, it was also a decade of fashion. For the first time in the 20th century, London not Paris was the centre of the fashion world. In the 60s, teenagers finally had the independence to dress differently to their parents. This report is going to explain how different the fashion was from the beginning of the decade to the end of the decade.

Boys and Girls

The early 60s fashion was completely different, especially for young boys and girls because colours and patterns were introduced. At the start of the decade, most parents couldn't afford decent clothing for their children so instead mothers would usually handmake their clothes. The girls clothing was very simple. They would wear a box dress with long socks and a simple ponytail in their hair. Boys on the other hand, would just wear a top and trousers, but as the decade went on, more patterns and colours were introduced to children expanding their range of clothes. For example, chequeredboard, stripes, polka dots and colourblock. These were later used on clothes such as suits, dresses, box dresses and much more.

OHHH

Women

From the early 60s, right through to the end of the decade, women's fashion was still as stylish as ever. Designers such as Mary Quant and Andres Courreges invented the most famous trends of the 60s such as the mini-skirt, crop tops, hot pants and bell bottoms. London had led the way with the Mod look since the late 50s, and continued to do so with the new styles. Models were also influential. For example, the model Anita Pallenberg was a fashion icon for bands like The Rolling Stones with her rock chick look, thigh high boots, fringing and skin tight prints. Make-up looks also changed and were at both ends of the scale, from the natural looks of the hippy brigade to the dramatic black and white eyes of Mod, with pastel colours being the most popular.

Men

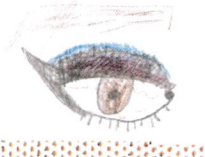

Men's fashion in the decade was just as varied as women's and ranged from smart suits to leather jackets. Going into the late 60s, men were allowed more freedom in what they wore because they were no longer required to do National Service (two years in one of the Armed Forces) and no longer needed to follow strict rules on their appearence. Usually men wore sports shirts with the polo style being the most favoured. Men's hairstyles varied throughout the decade. Long wavy hair was the hippy look and short cut hair was the Mod Look.

As seen previously, the 60s was a huge decade of change in fashion. Things invented that before were thought as being stupid and meaningless, were seen as the height of fashion by the end of the decade. Fashion from the 60s to the Modern day hasn't changed that much. Mini-skirts, crop tops and hot pants are some styles that are still worn today.

Ruby Watkins and Macie Cox

1960s

1960s Fashion

The 1960s was a decade of change especially in fashion. There was a huge variety of styles from the beginning to the end of the decade and everyone had their own unique styles. For the first time in the 20th century London, not Paris, was the centre of the fashion world. This report is about fashion in the 1960s.

Mary Quant

Mary Quant was arguably one of the most famous designers of the 1960s. Mary Quant's fashion shows starred mini skirts. The shorter the mini skirt showed how confident the person wearing it was. Mary Quant made small things like mini skirts and called it minimalism.

OHHH

Colourful materials

Another important change of fashion in the 1960s was how colourful the designs were becoming. Some of the different patterns were floral which was a flower pattern and trellis which was a chain pattern. In the 1960s, they used man-made materials such as polyester and nylon.

Men's fashion

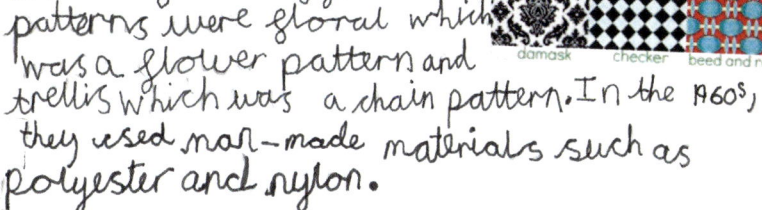

Men's fashion had just as much of an impact as women's fashion throughout the decade. Tie-dye shirts, long hair and beards were common place. Men and young boys wore tunics and capes and flared trousers. Flared trousers were the 60s version of trousers. Men in the 60s access accessorised with boots, bold bright shirts and sometimes high heeled boots.

OHHH

The fashion in the 1960s was different from today but there were also some similarities. Many fashions from the 60s are still around today such as mini skirts and hot pants. The fashion designers in the 1960s lead the way for new fashion designers today because it is easier to get into the fashion industries.

Isabel Pottle and Rebecca Clark

1960s Fabulous Fashion ???

The 1960s was a decade of change especially in fashion, music, art, leisure and television. Teenagers became more independent from their parents with different fashion interests and opinions. The beginning and the end of the decade were the complete opposite as life turned back to normal after the shortages of the Second World War had finally come to an end. Fashion was a massive part of the 1960s as, for the first time, London, not Paris, was the centre of fashion. This report is about the popular fashion trends of the 1960s.

Women's Fashion

The most popular clothing item for women's fashion in the 1960s was by far the mini skirt. However, there were many other unique styles. Women wore many bright, contrasting colours to match the current pop art and hippie trends. Dresses were shapeless with high neck buttons or turtle necks. Twiggy was an extremely famous style icon and model. Many clothes were invented by the designer Mary Quant. Their trousers were like a frilly dress as they were baggy with flared bottoms and got pulled high up the waist. Women were wearing geometric patterns and so were the men. There were rectangular bags as well, **normally** with a shoulder strap. Mary Quant designed the jumper dress along with the mini skirt and the length of the skirt depended on how confident the wearer was. If it was long it meant you weren't so confident; if the skirt was high, it meant you were **confident**. Popular shoes were: low heels, flats, Go Go boots which were worn in brown, silver and white vinyl. Popular clothes were: Mini skirts, jumper dresses, baby doll dresses, Mini shift dresses, Mod dresses, cocktail gowns, Maxi dresses and dress suits.

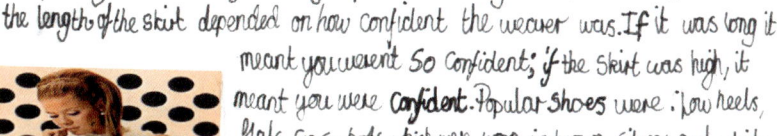

Men's Fashion

During the 60s mens lives had a dramatic fashion change from the 1950s. This is because they were no longer required to do National Service, so therefore had more freedom to explore new styles and haircuts. National Service was when men were in the armed forces in case there was another war. So they had strict rules about their appearance. Men started to grow their hair long and could experiment with new, different trends. At the beginning of the 1960s men's trousers became much slimmer on their legs, but towards the end of the decade they were flared at the bottom.

Haircuts

Haircuts in the 1960s weren't the style that most people would wear today, with their messy moptops and large afros, they were more outgoing. One of the most popular hairstyles for women was 'the beehive'. It was an exaggerated pinned bun with lots of hairspray to hold it upright. Another popular haircut for women was the 'flipped bob'. It was a short bob that flipped out at the end and was worn by Diana Ross and Jacqueline Kennedy. Hippie was such a common style in the 60s that there was a specific hairstyle for the trend. The hippie haircut was mid length and normally had some kind of fringe. The mop top' was popular as it was worn by the Beatles. 'The moptop' was a messy, longer hair and the hair moved away from the back. Italian designers took over Britain with their famous haircuts. Nearer the end of the decade men grew sideburns beside their long hair.

The 1960s had many similarities and differences from fashion in the present time. Although the 60s was some time ago, paisley patterns, headbands, peace signs and sandals are still common in many places today. Women wearing mini skirts still continues to be a trend for many. The hippie style, which was a common style for both men and women, is considered being vintage and eccentric, so has become a costume party favourite. In years to come the 60s should influence more unique styles and trends.

OHHH

Girls (sketch labels): The flipped bob, red lipstick, necklace, bracelet, glossy dress

Boys (sketch labels): Combover, suit, skinny tie, grey shirt, buttons, blue trousers, high heels, high heeled boots

- Many people wore patterns such as the Jumbo Dot. It was a large Polkadot pattern that was often used on dresses.
- Many people started wearing different tights in a variety of colours that they found more exciting than tan coloured tights.
- Mini Skirts weren't just a popular fashion choice but a symbol of womens rights to show of their bodies.

Saranya Lister and Jesse Cummins

OHHH GROOVY

Fab 60s Fashion

The 1960s was a decade of many changes especially in fashion when everybody wanted that "must have" item of clothing. There were many different styles and everyone had their own look. From the beginning to the end of the decade, music became a big influence on fashion. The musicians wore some very weird fashions!

Women's Fashion

In the 60s there were many changes and different styles of women's fashion. Women had an alternative look to the men because most men liked to dress smart whereas women's styles varied. For example; smart, hippy, mod, colourful and riders. Mary Quant was one of the biggest designers. She invented the mini skirt. The shorter the mini skirt, the more confident the woman was. Women wore trousers that flared out at the bottom called flares. Headresses also became fashionable.

OHHH

Men's Fashion

Men's fashion was just as varied as women's and changed a lot as well. In fact men wore styles that influenced women to wear the same. Men's style had particular products such as parkas, flared trousers, leather jackets and ringo ties (a skinny tie). The reason why men's fashion changed so much was because National Service (two years service in one of the Armed Forces) ended and men didn't have to keep to strict rule about appearance any more.

Hippies

In the 1960s, the hippy style was very different from other day to day fashion. Hippies, whether they were men or women, wore their hair long. They dressed in flowery ponchos which are still around today. Tie-dye t-shirts, with their distinctive circles, were also popular.

As can be seen, fashion was very different in the 1960s than it is now. Although fashion designers today have new ideas, some styles from the decade such as ponchos, parkas and mini skirts, are still around today. Fashion in the 60's had a huge influence on clothing today. Women still wear flowers in their hair (especially at music festivals) and many men continue to wear polo shirts.

Benjamin Coles   and   George Reynolds

60s Music

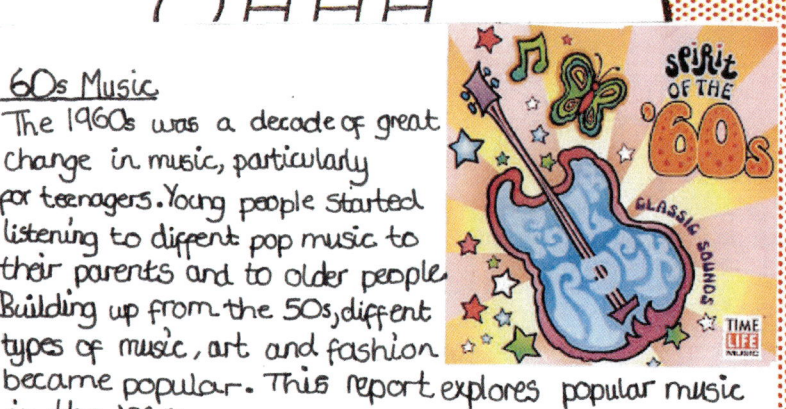

The 1960s was a decade of great change in music, particularly for teenagers. Young people started listening to diffent pop music to their parents and to older people. Building up from the 50s, diffent types of music, art and fashion became popular. This report explores popular music in the 1960s.

The Animals

The Animals were a pop, rock and rhythm band formed in the 60s. They were the rock band most influenced by black Americans rather than the Blues. The Animals were formed in Newcastle, and later found fame in London in the middle of the 60s decade. The names of some songs that they sang were 'The God Spell' 'The House of the Rising Sun' and 'Don't let Me Be Misunderstood'. The Animals got into the Hall of Fame, In the late 1960s.

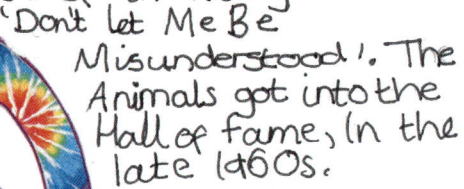

OHHH

The Beatles

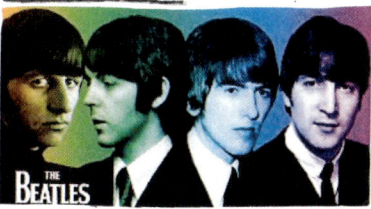

An even more popular band than The Animals were The Beatles. (John Lennon, Ringo Starr, George Harrison and Paul McCartney). They were known as the 'fab four'. The Beatles sold a smashing 600 million albums (the most in the world) However, not all of their songs were a hit or had catchy lyrics to start with. For example, the first lyrics to 'Yesterday' were 'Scrambled eggs!'. Places from their childhoods influenced their songs for example, John Lennon grew up near a place called Strawberry fields in Liverpool which was a children's home and he played in their garden.

The Kinks

Another English rock band, formed in Muswell Hill, were called The Kinks and were on of the most influencial rock bands in the 60s era. Their band emerged during the height of British R&B (Rhythm and Blues). The Kinks amazingly realeased 28 albums in the UK but their third single that Ray Davies penned, 'You really got me', became an international hit. The group released a string of hit singles and studio albums.

OHHH

As seen previously, music was very popular in the 1960's and still is today. Bands and artists from the 60s influenced many other artists to create new sounds of their own. For example, Liam Gallagher who was in Oasis has been inspired by The Beatles. In addition, artists such as the Rolling Stones and The Who, are still touring and selling albums. This shows what a massive influence music in the 1960s.

Interesting facts

Top 10 decade songs:
1. I Want To Hold Your Hand, The Beatles 1963
2. All Along The Watch Tower, Jimmy Hendrix 1968
3. (I Can't Get No) Satisfaction, The Rolling Stones 1965
4. Good Vibrations, The Beach Boys 1966
5. My Generation, The Who 1965
6. Like A Rolling Stone, Bob Dylan 1965
7. Respect, Aretha Frankling 1965
8. You Really Got Me, The Kinks 1964
9. Mrs. Robinson, Simon & Garfunkle 1968
10. Hit The Broadway Jack, Ray Charles 1961

Lilly Hebdon, Martin Sawdy and Jake Addicott.

The 60s music

Five decades ago it was a decade of change, the 60s. There was fashion and other glamorus stuff such as pop art, controversial movies and people had diffrent ways to spend their time. The music was 'cool' and 'groovy'. This report is about diffrent types of music in the 1960s.

Pop music

One of the most famous pop bands in the 60s was The Beatles. Formed of John Lennon, Paul McCartney, George Harrison and Ringo Starr, they were created in Liverpool in 1960. The Beatles released their first album called 'My Bonnie' in 1961. They were known as the 'Fab Four'.

Another popular pop band in the 60s was The Beach Boys. Brian Cone of the Beach Boys quit the tour in 1965 because he was tired

They never sang alone because they were always a team.

Rock music

Rock music was one of the most popular types of music in the 60s. The Rolling Stones were by far one of the most popular bands. The Stones started in London in 1962 with Brien Jones, Mick Jagger, Keith Richards, Billy Whitecamp and Charlie Watts. The Who (another band) always smashed up guitars and kicked over the amp. They were most famous in 1963 because they released one of their best selling albums, 'Tommy'.

Country music

There was also Country music in the 1960s. Johnny Cash made lots of popular Country music. Johnny Cash, who sold million of albums, was born in 1897. Patsy Cline (1932-1972) also sold millions of albums. Patsy Cline was the first woman to perform at New Yorks Carnegie Hall. Patsy's first album was called 'Walking After Midnight'. The most copies of a single she sold was 832,003 with 'I fall To Pieces'.

OHHH

Music in the 60s was more popular because records were cheaper. Nowadays, music is available in diffrent ways other than records (downloads, livestreaming and CD but can be expensive. Also, the conserts are hard to get into because everyone wants to go - although many people find it difficult to afford them. Conserts today are very diffrent than the 60s because sound equipment is much improved and there are effects like big screens so you can see the stage from a distance, and light shows.

	1960s	2017
	Help	Despisito
	Baba O'rily	Attension

Arthur Jones,
Josh Pearce
and Lenny Raw.

OHHH 60's Music History

The 1960s ('The Golden Era') was the start of many new trends. There were lots of varied styles of music from the beginning of the decade to the end. During the 60s, young adults and teenagers began to develop different opinions to their parents which was shown in artwork, fashion and music. This text will expand on the knowledge of 1960s music.

Styles Of Music

1960s music differed hugely in style and genres. One of the genres was R&B (Rhythm and Blues) which was a soft gentle style of music. There was also Motown, Folk, Soul, Rock and Jazz. Some popular hits from Motown included 'Baby Love' by The Supremes, 'I Can't Get Next To You' by The Temptations and '(Your Love Keeps Lifting Me) Higher And Higher' by Jackie Wilson. Some Rock songs were called 'Paint It Black' and 'Satisfaction' by The Rolling Stones and a Soul song by Dusty Springfield was 'I Only Want To Be With You'.

English Bands And Artists

Throughout the decade, lots of exciting English musicians and

OHHH

groups were appearing with new styles of music. The Beatles' first American concert was in the Washington Colosseum on February 11th 1964. The Beatles started 'The Hippie Revolution' and sung a mix of Pop, Rock and R&B. Also, their best selling album was 'Sgt. Pepper's Lonely Hearts Club Band'.

The Rolling Stones have been going for roughly 55 years and are still going now. A film maker called Brett Morgen made a documentary on them for their 50th aniversary called 'Crossfire Hurricane'. Other musicians and groups included The Kinks, The Who and Dusty Springfield who started out in a folk trio and then became a Soul Singer.

How Music Evolved

In the 60's, many musicians and groups mixed different genres of music to create new sounds. One of the groups to do this was The Beatles. At the end of the 60's, their music sounded completely different to the start because they were mixing rock pop and a hint of R&B together. The Beatles visited India for inspiration on music from different cultures. Overall, teenagers influenced bands to experiment with new music by having different tastes to their parents.

OHHH

Many records were made in the 60s. Despite them being around 50 years old, they are still listened to today. Some bands and artists in the 60s are still performing live gigs and create music today. A few of these include The Rolling Stones, Paul McCartney (from The Beatles) and The Who.

60s

Facts

- 'Crossfire Hurricane' (The Rolling Stones' documentry) was named after a lyric in one of their songs called Jumping Jack Flash.
- Top Five Artists (in order)
  - 1 - The Beatles
  - 2 - The Rolling Stones
  - 3 - Bob Dylan
  - 4 - The Beach Boys
  - 5 - Jimi Hendrix

Nancy Black and Eliza Pettit

Music in the 1960s

The 1960s was a decade of change, especially in music, as teenagers realised that they didn't have to be like their parents. The younger generation found their voice and found that they had different tastes in music than the older people.

The Beatles

By far one of the most famous bands in the 1960s was The Beatles. They were John Lennon (vocals), George Harrison (guitar), Paul McCartney (bass) and Ringo Starr (drums). The Beatles formed in The Cavern club in Liverpool, playing covers in the 1960s and split up in 1974. Their first hit single was 'Love, Love Me Do'. Also, The Beatles sold over 600 million albums; the most in the world ever.

Did you know? The album cover of Sgt Pepper had lots of famous people on the front such as Winston Churchill, Nelson Mandela, Brunel and Martin Luther King Jr. Ringo Starr's real name was Richard Starkey

THE BEATLES

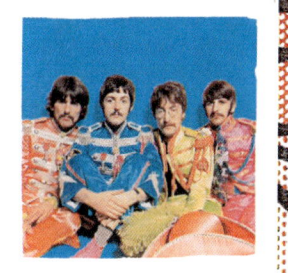

The Who

Another popular music group in the 1960s was The Who. They were made up of Roger Daltrey (vocals), John Entwistle (bass), Pete Townsend (guitar) and Keith Moon (drums). They were four London mods who

OHHH

Smashed guitars, over turned drum kits and wrecked hotel rooms. Even though they did this, they produced rock tracks, had five world wide number ones and sold over 150 million albums. In Britan, The Who had over 40 number ones.

> **Did you know?** The Who once wrecked a hotel room that was worth 200 thousand pounds! Top 5 Who Songs: 1.'My Generation' 2.'Substitute' 3.'I Can See For Miles' 4.'I Can't Explain' 5.'Pictures of Lilly'

The Beach Boys

The Beach Boys were massively popular in the 1960's particulary in America. Although the Beach Boys had many members in the band, Brian Wilson was the most influential because he wrote the songs, sung them and was experimental with different types of music. In the year 1964, Brian Wilson suffered a mental break down but survived the ordeal.

> Top 5 Beach Boys Songs 1.'Surfing Safari' 2.'Surfing U.S.A' 3.'Little Duece Coupe' 4.'Fun, Fun, Fun' 5.'I Get Around'

The BeacBoys

Even though most music is more computerised than 1960's, some bands are influenced by the music and the techniques of bands in the 1960's for example Oasis were influenced by The Animals and The Beatles.

OHHH

These are some of the top 10 artists of today and the 1950s. 1960s: 1. The Platters 2. Ray Charles 3. Ray Peterson 4. The Everly Brothers 5. The Ventures 6. Floyd Crammer 7. Duane Eddy 8. Johnny Preston 9. Brian Hyland 10. Frank Sinatra. Today: 1. Little Mix 2. Lady Gaga 3. Shawn Mendes 4. Clean Bandit/Zara Larson 5. Anne-Marie 6. Dua Lipa 7. Ed Sheeran 8. JP Cooper 9. Katy Perry 10. Rag N' Bone Man

Evan Ottery, Harrison Mustapa and Jack Chambers.

1960s Art

The 1960s saw more changes to art than any other decade previously. Art developed with different styles and colours. The 60s art was more colourful than before and had an influence on many things such as fashion and music. Many adults and teenagers liked the change of artwork and styles. This report is about the impact of art and artists in the 60s.

Andy Warhol's adventure

Andy Warhol was by far, one of the most popular artists in the 1960s. He created the most famous print ever to be made and that print was called 'Triple Elvis'. Andy Warhol was born in Pennsylvania, 1928 on August the 6th. Just like any ordinary boy, he started school at the age of 4 and then went on to highschool and then college. Andy Warhol was famous for pop art (which means popular art). His picture of Marilyn Monroe was a beautiful print that had different neon colours such as pink, yellow and blue on it. It was probably one of the most famous images of pop art.

Jasper John's story

Jasper Johns was also a significant artist in the 1960s. He was born in Augusta,

Georgia in 1930 and, even as a small boy, he always hoped of being a famous artist. One of his most well-known paintings was the American flag. He also made a flawless painting of the U.S.A map.

Jasper Johns

Flower Power and The Hippies:
Peace in the world

In the 1960s, not just artists created art. Other people showed their creativity. For example, The Hippies made Flower Power art. On October 21st 1967, The Pentagon Washington, DC found itself surrounded by fifty thousand people protesting against the U.S military action in Vietnam. The flowerpower and the Hippies created lots of banners, tye dye shirts and art on cars. They also made flower designs and wrote peace and love on everything. The Hippies started in between the 1960s and 1970s and then went on to Canada, Britian.

Arts in the past

As shown previously, art started to evolve in the early 60s and is still popular today. Most of that art is still being sold but for millions of dollars and pounds today.

OHHH

For example, Warhol's 'Triple Elvis' sold for $81.9m in 2014. A variety of artwork took place in the 1960s and today, people still have this art hanging in their houses which proves they are still popular today.

Poppy Friedner and Megan Marriott

Andy Warhol died on February 22nd 1981

Hippies wore long colourful clothes and a peace necklaces

Jasper Johns has made some of the most popular art in the world.

Art in the 60s

The 1960s was a decade of great change for the Art world because usually paintings were realistic rather than abstract. It wasn't just a big influence on art it was also a huge impact on other popular cultures such as music, fashion and leisure. This decade was the big takeoff of the teenager. When teenagers decided to separate from what their parents liked and started to have their own image and way of life. It had an effect on art because artists wanted to have their own original style so they started to experiment with different styles. This report casts an eye over 1960s art.

Andy Warhol

Born on August 6th 1928, Andy Warhol took the world by storm with his new style of abstract art. This type of art was called Pop Art. He was part of the Pop Art Movement with Jasper Johns, James Rosenquist and Roy Lichtenstein. Some of his most famous pieces were 'Campbell Soup Cans', a series of 'Marilyn Monroe', 'Triple Elvis' and 'Che'. One of his previous jobs was as an advertisement illustrator for 'Glamour Magazine'. After he joined the art business, Andy Warhol won frequent awards for his unique style of art. On February 22nd, 1987, in New York he died aged

OHHH

approximately 53 years old, but his art still continued to sell for millions.

Roy Lichtenstein

Another artist who was involved in the Pop Art movement was Roy Lichtenstein. Roy was brought into the world in 1923 in New York. He caught the eye of the public with his comic book inspired pieces of art. A few of his most known pieces were 'Drowning Girl' and 'Whaam!'. 'Drowning Girl' was a Pop Art picture of a girl drowning and saying 'I don't care, I'd rather sink than call Brad for help!' and was made to look like a scene from a comic book. This was his first ever painting which was created 1961. One of his paintings (Nurse) was sold for $95.4 million dollars. Roy Lichtenstein died in 1997.

'Drowning Girl'

Bridget Riley

Compared to other artists in the 60s Bridget Riley had a very different style of art called Op Art. It involved optical illusions and mainly black and white were used to create them. Op Art looked like something was moving, flashing, warping or swelling and sometimes hidden images could be revealed. Born in the UK 1931 Bridget Riley flew to fame with her unique approach to art.

'Fall'

OHHH

She was most famous for her piece called 'Fall'. 'Fall' was made up of black and white wavy lines. Before she became an Op Artist, Bridget Riley did pointillism of mainly landscapes. She is still living to this day so is now approximately 86 years of age (1931-2017).

To this day art created in the 60s is being sold for millions. For example, 'Triple Elvis' (created by Andy Warhol) was sold for $81.9 million dollars in 2014. This decade had an influence on art today because it created a path of freedom enabling artists to express themselves. Modern art shows similarities and differences to art back in the 60s as they are both quite abstract. However, modern art can be as simple as drawing a dot on a page such as Kazmir Malevich's 'Dot' which sold for $60 million dollars.

Fact Box

- Bridget Riley's work may cause motion sickness
- Roy Lichtenstein started as a Cubist Artist
- Art critics severely called him a copycat
- Roy's son drove him towards Pop Art
- Andy Warhol's parents were immigrants from Slovakia
- Andy's actual name was Andy Warhola
- Bridget Riley used to be a teacher and worked in a glass shop.

Rebecca Gee and Anna-Lilja Tholozan

Mrs Reynold's Class; 5R

From left to right in both pictures.
Top row: Mr Faint, Samuel, Zachary, Bailey, Amber, Ellie, Ashton, Toby, Luke, Mrs Reynolds
Middle row: Christopher, Tia, Isabelle, Sophie, Abigail, Erin, Isabella, Vishal, Matthew
Sitting: Ben, Brandon, Lewis, Elliott, Sophie, Emily, Emma, Charlie, Archie, Rex

Music In The 1960s

Music in the 1960s varied from slow, quiet, gentle songs to loud, rock songs. Unlike today's musicians, people moved from band to band creating new bands as they went. In the previous decade, children were forced to listen to what their parents listened to, but when the year 1960 came, children began to have their own tastes and ideas. People's tastes developed as new bands came about and new songs were produced. Many bands, such as The Beatles and The Monkees had television shows based around them because people wanted to know more about what they did in their spare time.

The Beatles

The Beatles were the most popular band between 1962 to 1965. John Lennon and Paul McCartney met in 1957. Shortly after George Harrison and Ringo Starr joined, completing their band. After forming their band, in Liverpool, 1960 the 'Fab Four' (which is their nickname) soon shot fame with their first album. The Beatles are a great example of how they developed their songs to suit people's tastes. They went from 'I Want To Hold Your Hand,' a slow basic song to 'Lucy In The Sky With Diamonds' a loud psychedelic song. Sadly, John was shot in New York and George died of cancer,

OHHH but Paul and Ringo are still alive today.

THE ROLLING STONES

The Rolling Stones, who were an English band, formed in 1961 by Mick Jagger, Keith Richards, Ronnie Wood, Charlie Watts and Bill Wyman. They had their first concert on the 12th July 1962 at the Marquee. In January 1963, they released their first album. They mainly played rock songs on guitars and drums. The Rolling Stones fought against The Beatles constantly for first place in the charts, however The Beatles were number one between 1962 to 1965.

THE BEACH BOYS

Another band, The Beach Boys, formed in America but became popular in Britain in 1962. The Beach Boys consisted of Mike Lore, Al Jardine, Bruce Jonston and Brian Willson. They sang rock and their most famous album was 'Surfin' Safari'. They played on guitars and drums. In concerts, they regularly danced to their music using the swim — which is an old dance move used a lot in the 1960s. The Beach Boys most popular song, in 1967, was 'California girls.'

As seen previously, in the 1960s there was a wide variety of music. These days, music is

OHHH

as varied and as popular but has changed a lot. As we still have rock and opera but rock music is less popular than it was in the 60s. We now have rap music, which didn't exist in the 1960s. The 1960s music has influenced many current artists, for example, Liam Gallagher, formerly of the band Oasis said, 'The Beatles' were an inspiration for his music. People moved from band to band creating new bands unlike todays musicians who would leave and set up for themselves.

EMMA BUTTERFIELD AND SOPHIE PARKER

OHHH
1960s Art

Pop art was very famous in the 1960s. It began in Great Britain but quickly moved to New York City. It is another word for popular art. It began on a small scale in the 1950s but as the 1960s came along pop art grew popular because artists wanted to make art for the masses and some used it poke fun at tradional art. Some of the most famous pop artists were Andy Warhol, Roy Lichtenstein and Jasper Johns. Some types of art used famous images and incons, such as products from stores E.G Soup cans.

Andy Warhol

Andy Warhol lived from 6th August 1928 - 22nd Febuary 1987. He made art that used pictures of famous people (celebrities) and products that you would have seen in supermarkets, for example his use of Cambells soup cans. He also used lots of bright colours such as, red, white and blue. Andy Warhol created a picture of Elvis Presly, his image was repeated eight times heading to the right overlaping each other. The painting famously sold in 2009 for $100000000.

Roy Lichtenstein

Another famous pop artist, who was American, was Roy Lichtenstein. Lichtenstein made his paintings have the effect of a comic page. He made his paintings into comic-like images by using a variety of different sized dots. Roy also used the effect of onomatapoeia such as

OHHH

wham, boom, bang, hiss and pop. Two of his famous paintings were named drowing lady wich showed a lady drowing and wham (two planes shooting each other).

Jasper Johns

Another iconic artist of the time was Jasper Johns, who was also a sculptor and was born in 1930 Augusta Georgia. Jasper started drawing when he was very young, he would paint over a collage of newspaper or images from magazines. His best known painting is called flag and its based on the American flag. He has painted pictures in the pop art style and sold them for lots of money. In 1949 he moved to New York City to study at the Parsons school of designs. After arriving in New York he was drafted into the army. The owner of an art gallery (Leo Castelli) saw John's work when visiting Rauschbergs' studio and was impressed so much that he offered Jasper a job at his gallery.

The term 'pop art' came from a British museum superviser called Lawerence Alloway, from the phrase 'popular art' meaning art which a modern feel. Pop art is a style of art that is described as simple. It is meant to be fun using bold bright colours. As shown pop art was introduced in the mid 1950s in Britain, and then in the late 1950s moved to New York. This report has only covered some of the most famous pop artists of the 1960s who's art is still enjoyed by many today.
Archie Newby, Zac Southcombe, Vishal Balagopi.

Fashion in the 1960s

Fashion was very different in the 1960s. Clothes and styles were very colourful, vibrant and more exciting than today. In previous generations, children had followed in their parents footsteps but teenagers started to wear whatever they wanted. Women showed more skin than ever before by wearing crop-tops and shorts that looked like they had been cut from jeans into shorts. Rockers wore scruffier clothes, for example, black leather jackets and jeans. With black leather boots.

Clothes

In the 1960s mini-skirts were very popular and women liked to wear them. Music inspired people to design bikinis in 1963 after it was featured in the musical Beach Party. People in the 1960s dressed in bright colours and fascinating patterns. Bell-bottoms, tye-dyes and paisley prints became popular in the hippie-phase (which was in the mid-sixties.)

Shoes

During the 1960s, women wore comfortable shoes which were cheap and had very small heels. Some of the popular shoes were, for example, T-straps, sling-backs and loafers. Shoes for men had an enormous variety of styles and colours. Moccasins became popular during the late 1960s and were designer versions of the hippies style. The Moccasin was a shoe made from one piece of

OHHH

material drawn up and around the foot. Sling-backs had a strap that crossed behind a heel or ankle. A sling-back strap was similar to an ankle strap.

Make-Up!

The 1960s was a youth oriented decade. The baby-boomers were coming of age defining a decade of their own, through the use of make-up and hairstyles. Women wore very fun colours of make-ups for example, blue and purple, and we normally see the colours black and silver.

Men and Women's casual clothing in the 1960s was very colourful and vibrant. The fashion now is more settled and not as fun and crazy. Models such as Twiggy and designers like Mary Quant became icons. People had the confidence to wear whatever they wanted, just as they do now. Shayna Clark-maisiri, Rex Crolla, Erin Mitchell.

OHHH

Music in the 1960s

The 1960s was a time of innovation and excitement. Many new styles of popular music developed after the Rock and Roll of the 1950s. There was low unemployment, so young people had more disposable income to buy records and clothes and to go out dancing.

Rock Artists

Many British pop groups including The Beatles and The Rolling Stones were heavily influenced by the American rhythm and blues music. The Beatles, who included John Lennon, Paul McCartney, George Harrison and Ringo Starr, helped create a distinctively British sound which used British accents, different cord sequences and vocals, brilliant lyrics and rhythmic guitar cords. The Kinks also played an important part in the British invasion of music into American culture. Their early hits paved the way for the next decades of rock.

Popular Artists

Lulu Kennedy Cairns, better known by her stage name Lulu, was a singer songwriter who produced a famous song in the 1960s called 'Shout'. Petula Clark has been a star all her life. She has sold seventy million records with hits including 'Downtown' and 'I Couldn't Live Without Your Love'. Petula started singing at the age of seven made her radio debut at nine and appeared in the Royal Albert Hall at eleven.

Genres

Towards the end of the decade a mixture of genres had become popular. For example, Baroque Pop which combined rock with some elements of classical music. Sunshine Pop, which was a lightly produced subgenre of pop music that originated from Southern California. To appeal to preteens and teenagers Bubble Gum Pop had an upbeat sound.

As can be seen music from the 1960s had a big influence on the way people listen to music and many of these influences still exist today. For example The Beatles were at the height of their fame in the 1960s and many of their songs are still enjoyed around the world today.

Emily Gent and Isabella Bolger

Leisure in the 1960s

Leisure in the 1960s was mostly spent outside. Youth culture dominated the decade with flower power, which was a culture that marked the peace after the war. Children usually played outdoors with their friends so they got fresh air. More people had disposable income so families could access many leisure activities. These were beneficial because children were physically active instead of being inside watching television.

Social Activities

One thing both adults and children enjoyed was fishing, and having a mini contest to see who could catch the biggest fish. Children would go out with their friends and either ride bikes or just simply visit each others houses. People would go to their friends houses for a party or to just celebrate something, such as Christmas or a birthday.

Television

Most people had a television by the end of the decade, but they only had three channels (BBC1, BBC2 and ITV). Coronation street (which is still around

OHHH

now) first started at the start of the decade (1960). BBC 2 went on air in 1964 and was the first channel ever to broadcast in colour. Doctor Who, which was the first TV series to be aired on BBC 1, was first shown in 1963.

Family Activities

Many leisure activities in the 1960s were similar to those of today. The introduction of the working week, provided workers with allocated time off, allowing families to spend more time together. Common family pursuits were: Trips to the beach, going on bike rides, climbing trees in a wood, swimming and going on holiday.

The 1960s were a decade with many leisure activities. Many of the activities are still around now, such as hide and seek and tag, or 'it'. Many people enjoyed all of these things and still do today.

Christopher van der Ryst and Brandon Hall

OHHH

1960s Music

Music from the 1960s was influential and changed the way people viewed and interacted with music and musicians. In the 1960s there were lots of different types of music, for example, Rock, Motown and Pop. There was high employment so people had more disposable income to spend on records and going to clubs.

Motown

In the late sixties Motown started as a Detroit based record label, soon, it turned into much more as acts gained popularity around the world. Two of the most popular groups who came out of Motown were Smokey Robinson and the Miracles and Diana Ross and the Supremes. Both of these groups had as much chart success as any of the Rock groups that dominated during the sixties.

The 'British Invasion'

The 'British Invasion' was the name given to to the period of time in the early to the mid-1960s. During this time rock and pop from the United Kingdom became popular in the United States of America. One great band from the 1960s was the Rolling

Stones, who came out of England and performed their first single, which was a Chuck Berry cover. The Beatles were another famous English rock band, formed in Liverpool. Their members were John Lennon, Paul McCartney, George Harrison and Ringo Starr. They released many hits including 'Drive My Car', 'Help' and 'I Want To Hold Your Hand!'

Protest Music

Protest music was different to normal music because it's always had a political message. The Vietnam war spurred a protest movement. Songs were an important part. At the time folk music and protest music was connected to the 'hippies'. They brought awareness to the younger generations, who would then join the protest and grow the movement to persuade the government to stop the war.

As shown, music from the 1960s was influential and changed the way people viewed and interacted with music and musicians. There were a wide variety of music genres in the 1960s. This report has only covered a couple of them. The music from the 1960s is still widely listened to today. This shows that they were all great singers and bands, who have also influenced many artists we listen to today.

Charlie Heath
and Ben Chambers

OHHH

Fashion in the 1960s

Britain in the 1960s had an explosion of fashion. Bold geometric patterns became very popular. In the mid 1960s, the hippy movement emerged and brought a new type of fashion; tye dye, floral and a lot of free flowing clothing items. For the first time teenagers looked different from their parents because they gained more disposable income to spend on clothes such as those modelled by supermodels and designers for example Twiggy and Mary Quant. Mary Quant made alot of money from this.

People who influenced fashion.

By many, Mary Quant was considered to be the best fashion designer of the decade. She was born on the 11th of February 1934 in Blackheath London. In 1965, Mary Quant showed her new item of clothing the mini skirt (which then went on to be very popular with teenage fashion) in a fashion show. She invented hot pants which she displayed at her shop 'Bazaar'. For many years, Mary Quant worked with the model Twiggy. Twiggy was a famous model and was on the front cover of many fashion magazines. In the mid 1960s, Jacqueline Kennedy Onassis was the main fashion icon for women. She was born on 28th July 1929. Jacqueline wore pillbox hats, pastel suits, shift dresses, oversized sunglasses and pearls.

The men's main fashion icons were the Beatles. They mostly wore denim, turtle neck jumpers and suits. Also they had long hair and would often go to Bazaar to buy outfits for their girlfriends setting many trends for fans to follow.

Change in fashion

In the 1960s there was a colossal change in fashion. After World War II rationings stopped teenagers had more disposable income to spend (which meant they could spend more on clothes). Twiggy modelled many teenage fashion trends. She inspired teenagers to wear different clothing from their parents for example hot pants and mini skirts became so popular the name 'street fashion' emerged. In 1965 street fashion had to compete with a new trend the hippy movement. The hippy movement began because hippies wanted the Vietnam war to stop so the world could live in love and peace. Their fashion brought bellbottom jeans, tye dye and other long flowing clothing items such as gypsy skirts, fringed vests and blouses. Hippies had free flowing coloured hair which had many flowers in it.

Girls and boys.

Girls and boys fashion in the 1960s was very different from today and developed as they grew. Long dresses with matching shoes

OHHH

and hats is what babies would wear. A very popular clothing that babies would wear were sailor dresses and woollen baby grows. Throughout the decade girls clothes changed massively. In the early 1960s, girls would wear simple, earth tone dresses with very smart matching shoes and hats. By the mid and late 1960s, girls wore bold geometric, psychedelic patterns. Boys fashion didn't change much throughout the 1960s. Boys would wear turtle neck jumpers, flairs and bellbottom jeans. By the mid 1960s, teenage boys either became a mod or a rocker. Rockers (whose clothe choice was influenced by music) wore lether jackets, scruffy black jeans and rode motor bikes. Mods wore smart, simple, pastel suits and cared alot about their appearence.

It is well documented that fashion in the 1960s was very varied and had a lot of famous british models and designers influenceing choice. This report only covers the most famous fashion of the era. Today some trends from the 1960s are still popular for example, chequered shirts and patterned clothing items are worn more often than before. Also girls still wear sailor dresses but a lot of the trends have drifted out of fashion. The hippy movement broke out in 1965 and there are still hippies around today.

Abbie Norris and Sophie Gibbons.

OHHH

1960s Leisure

Young people in the 1960s were beginning to have more disposable income because rationing for the Second World War had ended in 1957. This, in turn, meant that people could access more activities. Dancing was becoming less formal as music was exploring other styles. As opposed to the classical music that had been popular in the previous decades. People listened to rock, pop and soul the most. Sport was becoming more accessible to the general public as the working week had been introduced, giving people more free time. Going to the beach became an increasingly popular social event.

Dancing

Dancing became an increasingly popular social activity. People wold go to dances more regularly and the concept of the disco (invented in France) had moved to England. Most dances were well known routines such as the 'Macarena'. Dancing was heavily influenced by music as the style would affect the speed and type of movement.

Sport

Sport (similar to now) was incredibly popular in the 1960s. The most frequently played included rugby, football and tennis. Badminton was another favoured

OHHH

sport in which players would hit the shuttlecock to echother to score points. In this decade, a Scottish team won the football European Cup and Graham Hill, a formula one driver, was victorious in three McClaren competitions.

Beach

The beach was a commonly visited place (more so than previously as the necessary transport was more available.). If people (particularly children) met friends at the beach, they would sometimes hold sand castle competitions. While children were playing in the sea, adults would be talking to friends or sat with a drink. Swimwear had also changed. In the past, swim suits had been from knee to neck, whereas the 1960s saw the emergence of swimming trunks and the bikini. Swimwear - like fashion - would incorporate bold, colourful patterns.

As can be seen in this report, people having more disposable income meant that they could access a range of leisure activities - a lot of which we still do today. This report has only covered a few of them. However, we use technology (such as portable devices) much more now than we did then. The 1960s showed dramatic change and influenced the activities of today.

Samuel Atkins

OHHH
1960s Cinema and Television

1960s cinema and television represented a decade of fashion and Rock and Roll. This decade was the birth of cinema when the general public moved away from theatre palaces and plays. Films in the 1960s became increasingly experimental and daring such as, 'Dr No' (the first James Bond film). By 1970 most households had a television. In Britain television was mainly in black and white until 1967 (the year colour was first aired).

Television

Television was popular in the 1960s as it meant that people didn't need to listen to the radio all the time. The BBC was instrumental in guiding the nations viewing. The organisation started showing programmes weekly such as Doctor Who (which was first shown on November 1963). Films began to revolutionise costume drama and BBC two became the first full colour channel in Europe (which was then extended to BBC one and Itv).

Cinema

A multiplex cinema was first built in 1962 (multiplex meaning multiple screen cinema). They were housed in specially designed buildings. Some multiplexes are regarded to as megaplexes. The difference between a megaplex and multiplex was the number of screens housed in the cinema. The largest of these would of had a capacity of thousands.

Spy, Science Fiction and Fantasy

Spy films in the 1960s extended by using sophisticated gadgets and worldly settings, for example, Goldfinger (a James Bond film). Science fiction and fantasy films used a wider range

OHHH

of special effects such as the Tardis (which is a police box used in Doctor Who).

As presented, there were a variety of films in the 1960s that are still popular today such as James Bond and Doctor Who. The difference between James Bond and Doctor Who in the 1960s and today are the advances in technology, settings and graphics. Despite these differences there are similarities including James Bond's iconic Aston Martin prop and the Police box (Tardis in disguise) from Doctor Who which were introduced in the 1960s and are still used today.

Elliott Scrier Lewis Mansfield

OHHH
Magical Music of the 1960s

Music in the 1960s was very popular. The genres were varied from rock, soul, surf rock and pop. The top two bands were The Beatles and The Rolling Stones. Both of them had over three million listeners.

Chubby Checker

Chubby Checker was very popular in the 1960s. He was born on the 1st June 1941. Also, he moved away from Spring Gulley and went to Philadelphia for three years and came back to Spring Gulley. Chubby Checker was an American singer. His real name is Ernest Evans. He was known for making the twist dance style more popular. Chubby Checker has recently been the voice in the oreo cookie adverts.

The Beatles

The Beatles were a very popular English band. They were formed in Liverpool in 1960. Their names were John Lennon, George Harrison, Paul Mccartney and Ringo Starr. In 1962 The Beatles were signed up by a producer, George Martin. Also, in 1975 Paul and John wrote films, songs and albums. One of their songs was in a film called the Yellow Submarine. Sadly, their manager passed away in 1967. Also, John got shot in 1980 and George died of cancer in 2002.

OHHH

Tom Jones

Another famous Welsh artist of the era was Tom Jones. He was born in 1949 as Thomas John Woodward. He was very famous during the 1960s and indeed is still listened to by many today. He has had a career spanning over 5 decades during which he has achieved many things including an Oscar award for best male artist.

As can be seen, the 1960 decade was fabulous for music. There were many artists who had over millions of listeners and also influenced different dance moves. Music today is pop and in the 1960s it was mostly rock.

By Ronnie Timms
and
Matthew Chambers

1960S

OHHH
Fabulous fashion of the 1960s

In the 1960s teenagers began to dress differently from their parents. This was a change from previous years. During this time the economic boom - that began in the previous decade - continued. As a result, that meant people had more disposable income to buy clothes with. Some popular fashion idols were Mary Quant, Jacqueline Kennedy Onassis, Brigitte Bardot, Mary Jane and Audrey Hepburn. The trends that emerged were bright and colourful.

Hair and makeup

In the 1960s hair and makeup was very different. By far the most popular hairstyle was a backcombed hair sprayed quiff, with a short fringe. Other styles also included a short bob hairdo. Most women added to this by wearing brightly coloured eye shadow with pink lipstick.

Womens fashion

Fashion in the 1960s was very different to how women dress now. The late sixties were the era of flared bottoms and geometric patterns. Polyester was a very common material used to make miniskirts. Sometimes the girls wore a blazer and knee length skirts. Alot of pshychedelic patterns were worn. Twiggy - whose real name is Lesley Hornby - was very popular and was famous for wearing polyester bright checkered mini dresses designed by Mary Quant. She was a mod icon.

Mens fashion

1960s men wore either a striped sports jacket, a smart blazer or a button up jacket. Occasionally, a bow tie was worn. Scuffed jeans were great for casual wear. With the abolition of national service for boys, mens hair trends were changing. By this time the hippy movement was encouraging a trend of longer hair - which was also being influenced by popular bands for example, 'The Beatles'.

As shown, the 1960s was a decade when teenagers began to start making their own fashion choices. There where a lot of fashion trends that where different to trends that happen now, for example, people wear skinny jeans instead of flared jeans/trousers.

Tia Humphrey and Ellie Saban.

OHHH

Leisure in the 1960s

Leisure in the 1960s was exploding! Leisure had always been popular but in the 1960s people had come up with a variety of new leisure activities. Some of these ideas were Barbie dolls, G.I Joe and children were often seen skateboarding along streets. The 1950s was different to the 1960s in many ways. For example, in the early 1960s the working week was introduced allowing many workers to spend more time with their families.

Sport in the 1960s

England saw alot of great sporting moments in the 1960s. In 1966, England won the football world cup final against West Germany. England also won the Rugby five Nations in 1967. In this competition the teams consisted of France, Scotland, Wales, Ireland and England. There were many famous football players during this time that are still remembered today. For example, names such as Pele, Bobby Moore, George Best and Lev Yashin.

Activities in the 1960s

Activities attracted growing numbers of people in the 1960s. Many more children were seen skateboarding for example. The scout movement in the 1960s reached over 3 million members. Families had more time to spend together because of the introduction of a working week meaning people had more time to carry out activities such as building planes and models. Pedal cart racing had been introduced in the 1940s but still in the 1960s it was popular. Many families raced carts in their neighbourhood. Less time was spent playing with technology because people had not yet created phones, ipods and gaming consoles.

Toys In The 1960s

Toys in the 1960s had a bigger variety than ever before. G.I Joe was introduced in the early 1960s and came in many different forms. Other toys were created in the 1960s largely because of the creation and wide use of plastic. Barbie was another popular toy at the time and many parents bought these dolls for their children.

As described the introduction of the working week affected how much time parents could spend with their children. They would have designated times off work in which they had more time to undertake leisure activities such as playing games, building planes and sport. These days, children spend more time with their phones, ipods and gaming consoles. Parents can also give themselves days off if they are ill or hurt. Parents still to this day carry out the same activities that they would have done in the 1960s.

Ashton Blackaby and Luke Bremner

OHHH

Rock Music From The 1960s

Rock music became a very popular genre in the 1960s. There were many different types of rock such as surf rock and psychedelic rock. While there were famous bands in America there were also popular bands in the UK, The Who (who had over 2.5 million record sales) and The Beatles (who had over 3.5 million record sales).

The Beatles

The most popular band in the 1960s (The Beatles) came down to London from Liverpool to record in a studio, in Abbey Road. They were the first ever band to be globally broadcasted on television in front of 200 million people in 27 countries! In 1963, their song 'Please Please Me' reached the number one position on the British charts for many weeks.

The Beach Boys

Another famous band from the 1960s were The Beach Boys, who came from California. Their songs (which were full of harmony and joy) were mostly about girls, cars and general teenage antics. There were five members of the band including; three brothers, their cousin and their best friend. For two years surf rock became a very popular genre. The Beach Boys were placed in the top 20 famous bands during the time of surf rock.

The Who

The Who (who were formed in London, 1964) consisted of Pete Townshed (guitar and vocals) Roger Darbey (Lead vocals), Keith Moon and Kenney Jones (Drums) and finally John Entwistle (bass).

OHHH

They started of by covering American songs and showcasing them. Some of their songs were 'I can see for miles', 'Pinball Wizard' and 'I'm free'.

Unsurprisingly, music in the 1960s made a big impact on the upcoming decades. We've only covered a few bands of that time, these are some more Cream, The Rolling Stones and Nancy Sinatra. Lots of people today listen to 1960s music rather than the present days music.

Toby Evans and Bailey Webb

Fashion in the 1960s

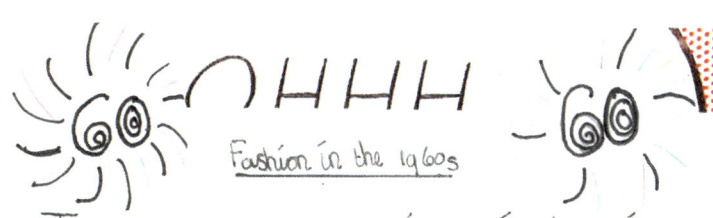

In the 1960s there were a variety of different fashion trends emerging. Young people in the previous years would have dressed like their parents but it was an exciting decade for everyone. Not only were designers such as Mary Quant and Mary Jane being quite innovative, the beginning of the super model era was happening with the use of Twiggy (who was very young but was known for styling clothes). Interestingly, at this time London was becoming the centre of the fashion world.

Clothes

In the 1960s clothes were very inventive. Women wore brightly coloured clothing that was very popular and stood out in the crowd. Dresses that people wore were very different to what people wear today because they were made out of crepe, shear and sheath. Men wore buttoned down shirts, jumpers and slim trousers, Pullover hooded tops for an athletic look as well as striped and checkered pullovers with many colours, which were also fashionable.

Hair Styles

During the 1960s there were a lot of different hair styles. Some of the styles were back combed, short curled, quiffs and buns. Mods hair was neat and tidy but not for Rockers. Their hair was messy and spiky. Beehives (another popular hair style) were mainly seen at dances. The hippies (another famous group) had their hair very long and parted in the middle. The Beatles influenced a lot of people with their hair style. Curtain styles were not as popular for men but were worn by young boys of the time.

OHHH

Make-up

Make up in the 1960s was very bright and colourful. Lip stick, eye shadow and mascara were the main components of womens make up. It was very glittery with pastel colours. Supermodels such as Twiggy wore attractive make up which encouraged lots of women to copy her style. A common style of make up was smoky eye, which starts of in the corner of the eye as a darker shade and fades into a light shade.

As has been seen, London was the centre of the fashion world. This report has only covered a few fashion models who would have been influencal in the fashion industry.

Isabelle Sukero and Amber Levy

VOGUE

Twiggy

Lippy

Year 6

'Was life better in the 1960s or today?'

Year 6 children have researched and written balanced arguments about whether life was better in the 1960s than in life today. They have compared and contrasted a range of features of society including: general life, school, music, leisure and environmental issues. Which view do you agree with?

Miss Gilliver's Class; 6G

From left to right in both pictures.
Top row: Elliott, Teddy, Jack, Olivia, Riley, Sam, Daisy
Middle row: Miss Gilliver, Amy, Grace, Scarlett, Lewis, Matthew, Ella, Ellie, Lily, Beth, Mrs Shropshire
Sitting: Donovan, Bill, Freddie, Jack, Ronan, Matthew, Samuel, Reggie
Bottom row: Caterina, Sophie, Amber, Lily, Libby, Evie

Was school life better in the 1960s than today?

Some believe that school life in the 1960s was better than today, but many disagree. In the 1960s, all the girls learnt sewing and cooking, whereas the boys learnt woodwork, but today, boys and girls learn the same things. At school now, computers and interactive whiteboards are used to help students and teachers, but at school in the 1960s, their method was 'talk and chalk' education: reading, writing and arithmetic.

Many people who lived through the 60s think that then was better because the children got free school meals. However, now (in modern times) parents have to pay for them. They also suggest that the 1960s was better because the schools got regular visits from the nit-nurse and the school dentist and that made the children healthier. They also got routine eye and hearing tests. Mr Polo (a child at the time) said that another reason school life in the 1960s was better was that there were stricter rules, such as: corporal punishments and lots of homework which made the children behave better. Furthermore, class sizes grew, which meant more children attended school.

On the other hand, many younger people disagree.

They think that modern times are better because punishments aren't physically harmful whereas in the 1960s they were. The children were caned by the teachers which led to terrified children and painful bruises. Furthermore, they argue that people in the 1960s had no classroom assistants to help in class, although now we do and it makes life at school a lot easier. They had no P.E kit. Instead they had to wear their vests and pants which was bad because the children got freezing in the winter, some people argued. The children of this generation think another reason was that the children in the 60s struggled in summer because there was no air-conditioning to cool them down.

In conclusion, one group of people think that the 1960s school life was better than today because classes were over 30 children. A further point they made was that children had free school meals. A different group of people disagree. They think that today's school life is better than the 60s because punishments aren't physically harmful. They also argue that in the 60s there was no air-conditioning or classroom assistants. What do you think?

Beth Barnes
Ella Cripps

Was fashion better in the 1960s or today?

After studying 1960s fashion and today's styles, it has been debated about which style is preferred. 1960s outfits were restricted to what they could wear, whereas now, there is a range of different outfits to wear due to cheaper clothing and richer welfare.

Many people argue that 60s fashion is much better than today's. Instead of today's relaxed and natural look, the 60s women pointed out that the bright bold colours helped them stand out. People who agree with this idea, also say that short skirts and mini dresses were also all the rage because of the popular model, Twiggy. This meant women felt confident with themselves. Moreover, the mod look included wearing massive hair styles and over-the-top accessories. 60s fashion followers, stated that this made them hugely popular people. Some others argue that hippy and rocker styles were more trendy than the mod look but the younger generation disagree. It is also important to note that most clothes were homemade because clothes were expensive; cheap imported clothes weren't available like today. People who lived through the 60s fashion trends say that this was better as it stopped so much manual labour.

On the other hand, many younger people claim

that actually, fashion today is much more popular. They state that modern clothes are much more comfortable and still stylish unlike the 60s, which seemed tight and ill-fitting. One point is that sports wear such as tracksuits, running leggings and vests are all worn nowadays as normal clothes as opposed to just for sports. This has proven to be better as is more comfortable for walking around. Furthermore, teenagers say that wearing trainers is much more practical than wearing heels all day. They also argue that the more neutral makeup look of today is better because of the garish bright colours and heavy makeup that was bad for skin.

In conclusion, it would appear no fashion is better than the other since they are two very different styles. Some still prefer the 60's fashion as opposed to the modern era looks, but what do you prefer?

Lily Smith and Libby Stratford

Was life better for children in the 1960s or 2017?

Lots of people are questioning whether life was better in the 60s or 2017. Now there are video games and smartphones whereas then, people were considered lucky if they had a landline (a home phone).

To begin with, adults who were growing up back then remember playing outside till dark; this gave them more exercise. They say that the streets were safer as there were fewer cars around than today. It is important to note that, nobody had to worry about homework and big tests like SATS. Adults who were children back then say that this was better as it caused them less stress. A further point is that music was very different. Adults say that it made the listeners feel more uplifted and happy. Music artists included: The Beatles, Cliff Richard and The Rolling Stones. Classics were created by artists who are still popular today.

On the other hand, people disagree and say that life today is better as there is more modern technology. Furthermore, this makes life easier as it helps complete everyday tasks like communicating and domestic tasks. A further point is that teachers are less harsh on their pupils by not using corporal punishment. This results in better work quality. The younger generation say that music is better today as it includes a lot of pop songs.

Overall, there are supporters of the decades who stand with different points of view. The question now is: who do you stand for?

Amber Cox
Lily Glenister
Riley Addicott

Was music in the 1960s better than it is today?

There is much debate regarding whether music from the 1960s is better than music that is produced today. In some people's eyes, pieces of music from the 60s have changed Britain's musical culture - not always for the best. While this may be true, everybody has a different view on music; what do you think?

Sixties music fans claim that music back then was better because more talent was required to make a great song. They say that this is because there was no such thing as electronic music so artists had to play their own instruments. Many bands and artists from that beloved decade are still going today which shows that the 60s music legacy is still going strong. These bands and artists include: The Shadows, The Rolling Stones and Cliff Richard. People from the sixties also claim that the variety of instruments that were being used in music at the time led to many great songs that give them the classic feel to this day.

While the older generation claim that music from the 60s was better than today's, the younger generation say the exact opposite. They claim that present day music is better because it is more popular and easier to listen to. They also say that today's music has a lot more genres, whereas the only thing they could listen to in the 60s was some form of rock. However (what with acapella's golden generation starting in the 60s), more genres certainly have been created with the enhancement of technology. These genres include: rap, hip hop, electronic and pop. Furthermore, with the invention of apps such as Spotify and Apple music, adults (and children) insist that music has never been easier to listen to and music videos make it much more entertaining.

It is clear that both eras of music are exceptionally good, with the 60s producing classics and present day music providing much more choice. It is definitely worth listening to songs from each time as they are all brilliant. There is only one question remaing now: which side are you on?

Bill Sherman Samuel Rice Turner

Was school life better in the 1960s than today?

School life in the 1960s was different than today. Some people argue that it was better in the 1960s. In the 1960s, they had a blackboard, whereas today they have a smart board.

The 1960s children claim that the schools now are better than the 1960s because school was stricter than today. They had things thrown at them such as: chalk, board-rubber and a ruler. Therefore, they were scared of doing anything wrong. Girls from the 1960s say that their skirt had to touch the floor. This was dangerous because they would often trip and when it was hot they would overheat. Last of all, teachers argue that teaching was worse because everything was hand-written, mentally worked out and had no electronics which was frustrating for the teachers.

Adults that were children in the 60s, say that the schools in the 1960s were better than today because children used to get hit by: a cane, ruler, chalk and a board-rubber so they could have a better behaviour and listen more to teachers. Adults who were children in the 60s, say that they were allowed to go home during lunch time. This was good because they could go and see their parents and it was cheaper. They also argue that as the nit-nurse and the school dentist visited the school, they made the children healthier.

In conclusion, looking at both views it would seem that they are equal. What do you think is best?

Matthew York and Reggie Hopson

Was fashion better in the 1960s than today?

There has been much debate over the past few years on whether or not 60's fashion is better than the styles of today. Many of the older generation prefer the trends of the 60s which include many styles, from mods and rockers to hippies, known by many as flower power. However, many of the younger generation prefer today's fashion.

To begin with, many women, alive in the 1960s, argue that today's style cannot even compare to the fashions from their youth. They claim that, for them, growing up was very different; the makeup was a major change. They point out, that compared to the 60s choice of eye makeup, the 21st century is more casual and made to look natural; before it, bright and bold, with eyeliner, was very popular. 1960s women explain that this meant people could express themselves and change their look dramatically through their choices of makeup. Others state that the hairstyles worn by Twiggy were far more stylish and they also argue that it was better because they had an inspiration to look up to, so they didn't have to worry about how they looked.

However, it is important to note that there have been many factual arguments against this. For example, the younger generation protest that the more laid back, comfy look is better. More precisely, sportswear such as: Nike or Adidas is hugely popular daywear and is better because it is far more comfortable than the tight mini skirts worn in the 60s. Another point teens make is that back in the sixties, trends were restricted to three styles: mods, rockers and hippies, whereas now, a great range of fashions are released almost every month, giving people a more expanded selection of choices.

In conclusion, it would seem that 1960's fashion override 2017's choice of style because trends tended to last longer; therefore it was cheaper as people didn't have to adjust their wardrobe as much as they do today.

Ellie Rice Turner
Evie Martin

Were children's lives better in the 1960s than today?

Life for children in the 1960s was very different to the modern lifestyle. This text will show the different views on living in the 1960s.

Adults that attended school in the 1960s say that they had a choice of whether they wanted to go home for lunch or stay at school and have school meals. This was better because the children could see their parents, and they didn't have to bring their lunch to school with them. They also insist that the 1960s were better than today; in Summer, the streets were undisturbed by cars. This meant they could play football as much as they liked. A supporting argument is that teachers were well thought of, so children got better education. Many of today's older generations state that most mothers did not work, so this was yet another advantage for 60s lifestyle. This meant that children could see more of their mum and do more activities together, which benefitted their health and learning. In contrast, as parents work almost every day of the week, it would be impossible today. Elderly people today argue that it was better as normally, children see more of one parent than the other.

However, no-one can deny the disadvantages of living as a child in the 1960s. Harsh punishments were given out by teachers: children had objects thrown at them; got the cane; and, on some occasions, the teacher would pick them up, turn them upside-down and dunk their head in the bin. Peter Bull, who was a child in the 1960s, states that children who got the cane often felt embarrassed, but it did not necessarily change their behaviour. Today, adults have argued that life is better for children now, one reason being that they have proper bathrooms. In the 1960s, children had to fill up a tin bath with a bucket and water, and move it in front of their coal fire. In other words, bathrooms are a lot easier to use today. To add to this problem, most of the time, children had to go outside if they needed the toilet; it was either outside (in the garden) or down the street. If children used the street toilets, they took paper with them — it wasn't provided in the toilets

Many people who were children in the 1960s claim that life was hard for them, as most of the time, they were at school or in the house doing chores. But there was always a bright side to that kind of lifestyle, as there was a lot more freedom and imagination involved than there is today, when most children are stuck to things like computers, games consoles and mobile phones. The real question is: who do you agree with on this?

Caterina Daffada
Daisy Ambridge

Was music in the 60s better than music today?

The 60s was a great decade for music, it was known as the decade of the British bands. But was music back then better than music today? Some people say yes, some people say no. Many opinions have proven that music today is just as good as music in the 60s.

1960s music fans claim that music back then was more smooth and jazzy than music today, so people could relax while listening to it. It it also important to note that bands and singers always had to perform live; this meant that they couldn't lip sync to a pre-recorded track like some artists do today.
Therefore, music sounded more authentic so if people wanted to do well in the music business, they had to have real talent, have the right equipment and practise regularly. A further point is, singles back then were number 1 for weeks and weeks whereas now number 1s only stay at number 1 for about a week because a new song is released by new artists very frequently.

On the other hand, people aged 10-35 have said that music today is better because back then, there were set dance moves for certain songs, whereas now you can dance however you want, to any music. Furthermore, people don't have to be good singers due to all the editing machines they have today. This gives artists an opportunity to perform. Artists today have said that it's easier to get a big break due to youtube, X Factor and BGT.

All of the facts for and against suggest that music today and music in the 60s are both good. But which one is better? Well, that choice is yours. Whose side are YOU on?

Jack Munt and Lewis Jerome Kimpton

Was school life better in the 1960s than today?

There was a lot of discussion between older people who had experienced life in the 1960s and younger people who experienced more modern school life today. Many things have changed including the punishments, technology and uniform. Many people debate whether the 1960s was better than 2017 because some of the experiences are different and people have different opinions.

The older generation claims that school life was better in the 1960s than it is today. They state that punishments were more strict than now. Punishments such as: the cane, a ruler across the knuckles and bits of chalk being thrown by the teacher at the children. They say it was cruel and painful for those who misbehaved. They also state that the nit-nurse (who was friendly) showed up every week for a healthy check up. As well as the nit-nurse, free sight and hearing check ups were provided for everyone because they could not pay.

There wasn't as much bullying as today which is good because people did not feel sad and left out.

However, others argue that 2017 school life is better. They say this because nowadays children are driven to school but back in the 1960s some children had to walk many miles to get to their school which would have tired them out. Adults say that because there is no corporal punishment nowadays, children aren't as intimidated by their teacher. Adults also state that P.E kits were more suitable for their age, rather than just their pants and vests as that is what they wore in the 1960s. With the improvement of technology learning has become easier; giving children the best education is what people need. At the moment 2017 is doing this.

To sum everything up, it is clear that these two time periods are both very different when concerning school life. What do you think?

Olivia Brant and Scarlett Porch

Was fashion better in 1960s or now?

There is a lot of debate whether 1960s fashion is better than today. In the 1960s, fashion was different than today. Many argue that trends were more defined and restricted because most ladies followed Twiggy who was a model. Whereas now, trends come and go and any clothes are acceptable.

Many people from the 1960s argue that fashion is better today than then. One reason is that clothes were uncomfortable and itchy; this was because most clothes used cheap manmade fabrics - as this was more affordable. Some people say that they dislike the style and trends because these were often tight fitting flares and unflattering shapes. Another reason that 1960s fashion was worse was the hairstyles and make-up: bee-hives, bobs, pixie cut, harsh make-up and false eyelashes. It is important to note that these were all trends that were hard to maintain.

Although there are strong arguments against the fashion from the 1960s, many people from that era think fashion was better. They liked clothing such as dresses and mini-skirts because of the mesmerising patterns. Arguing their point, they say that 1960s fashion was easier to follow because of distinctive trends, for example: hippies, rockers and mods.

After examining the different points of view, both trends have different pros and cons. What trend do you prefer?

Amy Fairfax
Grace Collins
Freddie Akers.

Was life better in the 1960s than today?

In the 1960s, school life was very different than today. Most people think that school life was better then; there weren't many cars around and less people worked. Whereas now, the streets are filled with cars and more people go to work. Some people suggest that the 1960s was better because children could do things like go home and have lunch but now children have it at school. In the 1960s, girls did needle work and cooking, boys did wood work. Whereas now they do the same things.

Many argue that school life was better in the 1960s; children got monitored at school for nits, hearing and sight. This was better because parents then had access and they didn't have to pay. Whereas now, it has changed because schools don't have nurses to check on the pupils. Another reason is, most children had free school meals (that meant parents didn't have to pay.) But some children were fed by their mums at home. Another difference is that children didn't have to take it to school. Some people think that the 1960s was better because now children aren't allowed to leave school; the streets are busier and it's not as safe.

On the other hand, many others have said that schools were not very well equipped because they didn't have any air-conditioning, nor did they have interactive whiteboards; they had blackboards instead. People who were at school in the 60s have explained that PE was awkward and embarrassing because they had to see everybody in their vests and pants. Children who were at school in the 60s, had very cruel punishments such as: a ruler over the knuckles; piece of chalk thrown at them; phone book thrown at them; a board rubber thrown at them and the Cane.

To sum up the points, most people have claimed that school is better now because punishment isn't as harsh as the 1960s; because children don't get canned or a ruler over the knuckles. Would you prefer the 1960s or now?

Sophie Bridgeman and Teddy Aves Ridley

Was music in the 1960s better than it is now?

It has been debated whether music was better in the 1960s or now. Some people think music is better now. Others believe it was better in the 60s. Music has changed a lot in the last 50 years.

It is argued by many that music during the 1960s was better than what is produced now. The main reason being that making songs required more talent due to the fact that artists couldn't make an electric sounding backing track. Everyone had to play their own instruments, thus creating a much smoother sound. Another reason why many older people argue that music was better in the 60s is that a lot of tracks from back then are still played today. Thus meaning that a lot of people still like 60s music and don't grow bored of it. Finally, music festivals were flourishing. As a result, there were a lot more chances for people to go and listen to their favourite bands. Music festivals now are extremely expensive compared to how much they cost in the 60s.

While many people believe that 1960s

music was better, music critics say that 60s music wasn't as good as it is now. One of the reasons being that none of the songs had a video to go with it. Many claim that it would be better if people could watch bands play music without having to watch a live programme. Another disadvantage of the 60s was that if people didn't want to pay to go and watch a band live it could be very difficult to listen to it because people would either have to listen on the radio or buy a record, which were expensive. Now there are apps such as Spotify and Apple Music where it is possible to download and listen to music in seconds.

In conclusion, it is clear that music from both times is amazing. In the 1960s, music was jazzier and smoother, containing classics that are still played today. On the other hand, songs from recent times are more upbeat with various sound effects and it can probably be argued that there are more songs out now than in the 60s. There are more genres now such as: hip hop, electronic and pop. It is definitely worth listening to music from both time periods. There is only one question remaining: Which do you prefer?

Matthew Tancock   Elliott Messenger

Was entertainment better in the 1960s than today?

In the sixties, entertainment was different compared to today. People didn't have access to the level of technology people have today, whereas today it covers most entertainment. So in the sixties, people had to find other things to entertain themselves. There's been debate on whether entertainment in the sixties was better or entertainment today.

Interestingly, Geoff Lightfoot, who was a child in the sixties, suggests that entertainment back then was better than today because children were allowed to play outside; whereas today children are stuck on computers. This means people are stuck inside and are not doing much exercise. Whereas in the sixties, people got outside which led to them getting more vitamin D. Heather Lightfoot says that children's entertainment was simpler but more enjoyable because on TV, when they could watch it, it was extremely random so they didn't see what was coming and thought it was really funny. The shows had funny character names and sometimes made weird noises.

Many of this generation claim that entertainment today is better than in the sixties. Technology was limited. So they didn't have things like: ipads, mobile phones, colour TVs, computers and game consoles. Today, all of this technology is played by adults and children alike. It's better today because there are more interactive things like: the internet, social media, video games, game consoles and mobile telephones. Barely anyone had a TV. This was bad because they couldn't watch things for entertainment. Back in the sixties there were no video games. Furthermore, many people could only communicate by letters but some lucky people could call others with landline phones.

So, some people think that entertainment was better some think otherwise. What do you think? Is entertainment better today or in the sixties?

Jack Lightfoot Ronan O'Reilly

Was School life better in the 60s than today?

Many things have changed since the 60s - inside of school and outside because of all the latest technology, teaching expectations and Ofsted. This debate shows that some people think that 2017 is better but others disagree.

The older generation have said that school back then was better because there were no electronic devices to help with learning; it was just heads down and learn whereas today, children are far too distracted to do so. They have also argued, that school life in the 60s was better because there was corporal punishment wich led to much better discipline. This made the children feel they wouldn't do it again (this was where children were physically hit by teachers). 60s pupils suggest that school in the 60s was better as there was no homework so they could be healthy and play outdoors with their friends. Also, it took stress off the children's mind.

Whereas, the older generation have said that having no homework is more suited for people, present teachers have argued, that having homework is much better education for children. Pupils are stuck on their computers so homework keeps them in the learning mindset. Present teachers have argued against the fact that the 60s was better because there were no electric devices, so present teachers believe that electronic gadgets in schools are much better for resources and information. The younger generation have spoken about the level of teaching. They claim that children now are much more clever because children now are learning what the 60s children learnt in secondary school.

In conclusion schools in the 60s and today are much different in various ways. As a result, everyone has their own experience of school. What do you think?

Sam Compton
Donovan Ahern

Mrs Thorne's Class; 6T

From left to right in both pictures.
Top row: Melissa, Jack, Callum, Luke, Emma, Maisie, Lydia, Noah
Middle row: Max, Maisy, Brooke, Jake, Mrs Thorne, Mrs Norris, Joe, Hannah, Josh
Sitting: Sam, Alexis, Archie, Sophie, Jimmy, Luke, Natasha, Jack, Dylan, Kieran
Bottom row: Abigail, Zachary, Josh, Mia

Was life better in the 1960s than today?

Nowadays, there is a lot of debate that life today is more advanced and better than the 1960s. There is no doubt that technology has progressed massively as well as being far more entertaining: phones, Ipads, laptops and gaming consoles. Schools point out that children have a more challenging curriculum and school learning is quicker and easier for the teachers as they use smart technology: smart boards, laptops and wireless connection. Others think that school was simpler in the 1960s as children learnt from textbooks. No one can deny that music nowadays is more varied as there are more radio stations and albums hold more songs. Rock concerts can also hold a larger capacity and more. Singers tend to take part in them. Others will argue music in the 1960s was better to listen to and made better money for the producers, as music couldn't be downloaded illegally.

There is no doubt that children's life in the 1960s had been spent mostly outside, playing games such as: hopscotch, hide-and-seek and tag. Supporters of music believe back in the 1960s it had been better paced and songs were upbeat where as now songs that get played are usually sad and slow. They further claim that at rock concerts it had been a better experience because the stadiums were up closer to the stage. Children were more creative as they liked to build model figures and kits that they could show off to their friends. Schools point out that children were less pressurised at school for quite a few reasons. No one can deny that SATs are far more pressurised now as teachers give kids a lot more homework and work them really hard. Back then the 11+ was less nerve wracking as they only told the children after the test that they had just done them. When he was at primary school, Mr Ballard learnt from blackboards, she said the teacher rolled down the blackboard and wrote on it with chalk and used a board rubber. In his leisure time, Mr Ballard liked to bike, build dens or if it was raining, he would play with his action figures. Supporters of the environment believe that less fossil fuels were released in the 1960s. Nowadays, many more planes and cars are running and releasing dangerous fumes; although in the 1960s less cars and planes were destroying the environment. They further claim that many more people cared for the environment, as it also helped the human race live.

On the other hand people believe that children's lives are far more enjoyable and have a lot more activities for them to do. It is widely believed that music nowadays is better than the 60s. There is no doubt that albums have improved massively over the years; more songs, different singers and more than one disc. Technology has hugely improved since the 60s. People have coloured television and there are many more TV channels so people can watch television of their choice. It could be argued that the amount of children of whom live in poverty has decreased immensely—due to a lack of jobs to choose from. In the 60s, more than half the population of children were living in poverty. Now only 20% of British children are currently living in poor circumstances. Schools point out that children nowadays are given a larger and better education. In the 60s children didn't have pre-school or even nursery, which effects not only the kids education but also made it harder for children to make friends, although now children can learn and make friends from a young age.

In conclusion, although it is widely believed that children

had more freedom and were less pressurised while being tested in the 1960s. There is no doubt that parents take better care of their kids and look out for their children now. Nowadays children are safer as when they go out they mainly have phones so they are contactable and they can contact other people. Children in the 60s didn't have this luxury.

Archie Ballard.

Was life better in the 1960's rather than today?

Nowadays, many people believe that whilst the advanced electronical industry is one of the best things in our modern day, others strongly feel that 1960's was a safer place for children. Supporters of 1960's being a better place, have argued that in the 60's kids were more sociable not only with their friends but with their families; as they were not always on their electronics. However there is a lot of debate that without electronics children would not be able to learn as well as they do now. Those in favour of the 1960's being better, argue that children were more free in the 1960's - as they were always out with friends -. Others say that kids are more interactive nowadays; but communicate differently to the 60's.

On the one hand, it is strongly believed that children were more sociable with each other in the 1960's. Children would pass their time by playing games such as: hopscotch, hide-and-seek and tag. When she was a child Miss. Clarke spent her free time by: going out on her bike, swimming in the local pool and playing in the park with friends. No one can deny, that in the 1960's children had more freedom, as parents were less aware of the dangers that roamed the streets. Also parents in the 1960's were ok with children being out alone as there were less cars. Although children were happy enough playing outside, when it was too cold and had to stay indoors; they would enjoy listening to music with their whole family. As he grew up Mr. Nash loved listening to the Rolling Stones and David Bowie; on his record player. Many people believe that in the 1960's that there was less pressure for children to look a certain way, to wear the right clothes; or to even act a certain way.

On the other hand, many others believe that whilst children may have met up with each other more in the 1960's; nowadays they have more friends that they socialize with frequently (on their electronical devices). It is more popular to go on social media now than ever before. Supporters of social media argue that: finding friends from all over the world — on these APPs — is extremly vital to building a child's social life. They further cite, that now parents are more aware of dangers that are out there, they are more protective over their children. In addition, the music industry has changed immensly since the 1960's; back then music was colossal but was only ever Jazz, Rock or soul, now music is more varied for different opinions.

In conclusion, many people believe that life in the 1960's was a better place for children: as they had more freedom and there was less pressure for kids to act a certain way, however it is clear that life is better now. People that believe this have argued that, nowadays it is more popular for people to set trends and for children to try them. Some of the trends are slime, make-up hacks and clothing hacks. However this doesn't mean that kids are being forced to do them. Furthermore, these people cite that children are not pressured to do anything and these trends are merely a bit of fun.

Hannah Nash

Was life better in the 1960s than now?

There was a lot of debate about some people believing that the 1960s were better than modern day. People who defend 1960s say that they were a time of safety and peace; a lot of people deny this and say that the modern days are better than the 1960s. Back in the 1960s, life was simpler but is simpler always better? The 1960s use of technology was rare, lots of people who defend the 1960s say that children use technology then take it for granted. It's quite unfortunate that people in the modern day 'specifically children' are told the phrase "We didn't have internet back in my day." It's just to stop children moaning really.

On the one hand, children had more freedom to do what they pleased in the 1960s. In their spare time children would be monitored-less, they would be able to go out in the street due too little-to-no cars. Children played games such as: skipping, hopscotch, tag and other socially popular games, to pass the time children nowadays would spend on their electronics. When she was younger, Mrs Hewitt would play with her dolls and ride her bike with her friends. Many people believed that children were under much less pressure, for example most children weren't told that they were doing their 11+ until they'd finished. Some experts argue that music was more popular than today, because the music was up-beat and lively which gave people a feel-good-feeling. People had to go out and buy vinyl or radios instead of downloading digitally.

On the other hand, it is widely believed that life for

children is now more efficient. Nowadays, children can spend their time on electronics, which can expand their knowledge. At school teachers often use interactive whiteboards. Teachers cite that it can help them quickly navigate through web-pages to find the class's work for that day. Also kids have access to Ipad and laptops to help; there are just more safety precautions that have to be met. Also music can be downloaded digitally instead of brought in shops.

In conclusion, now is more popularly thought to be better than the 1960s. Entertainment is now better with the quality enhancements of the shows and songs than the 1960s. Either opinion is valued and valid, either way. 2017 is better for children.

Melissa Hewitt, Jimmy Weatherall

Was life better in the 1960s than Today?

There is a lot of debate — all around the world — about whether the 1960s is better than now. There has been a lot of changes since the 60s; including school uniform. It could be argued that the uniform is much fairer now, for example: the uniform was much more restricted (the girls could only wear dresses and boys only shorts and trousers.) Back then, the children had much more freedom; nowadays kids parents are overprotective of their kids. In 2017 there are lots of childrens TV channels so thar is more choice, whereas back then there was only 1 hour of TV. At school there is much better equipment such as: whiteboards; interactive white boards; maths equipment and PE equipment. The punishments were much worse back then as kids got beaten.

On the one hand, many people believe that children in the 1960s actually had freedom and it was much safer. When she was younger Miss Taylor always played in the street and nearby woods. She played with dolls and played sports like tennis on the streets. She only had to come home when she was hungry. Back then children played games like hopscotch where they could socialise with friends; whereas nowadays all children have been taken over by technology. School was very different back then Miss Taylor remembers: being in the school choir; knitting socks and making people recite all of the times tables by yourself, infront of the whole class. It could be argued that there was no pressure at all on children but nowadays there is a lot of pressure on kids to do at school. Miss Taylor recalls doing a test called 11+ (instead of SATS) and the tests were so relaxed that they did the test and didnt even know it. In the 1960s, children were trusted to go home for lunch and then come back then school. No-one can deny that children from 2017 are becoming addicted to TV as there is so much to watch; in the 60s no-one had that problem as kids TV was only has on for 1 hour.

On the other hand, it is widely believed that life is much better now. Even though children don't have much freedom, kids play games like Tag and Cops and Robbers in the streets. Although there is a lot of pressure on kids now; teachers prepare them for tests so they get good grades. In 2017, children can't go home for lunch until they are 12 but there is much more lunch choices and now there is a vegetarian option. There is no doubt that children can get addicted to TV but there is much more choice. The TV now is much better because it is in colour almost all of the time. Also children can use a TV remote instead of having to heave their bodies from the comfiness of the sofa to turn up the sound or change the channel and and now there is much more genres and channels. They further claim, that children can now catch up now on TV shows if people missed them (if people have the right TV) all they have to do is press a button. Ask yourself, what do you think?

In conclusion, most people think that life was better in the 1960s as there was more freedom but it is obvious life is better now. In 2017 children might have less freedom but it is obvious life is better now. Children now might have less freedom but they feel more cared for; children do still play in the streets now but normally have contact with their parents by their phones. Others argue, there should've been a PE kit which they didn't have. Furthermore, children benefit from technology and having contact with friends at the tap of a finger. But what do you think?

Brooke Taylor.

Was life better in the 1960s than today?

There is a lot of debate over life in the 1960s being better than today; but is that really the case? Since the 1960s there has been a lot of changes even though some haven't made the right impact. Children are now reliant on technology and now struggle to do basic everyday tasks without it! Furthermore, people don't go out to buy vinyl records, they purchase CDs (or music from Itunes) and get it delivered. Children are becoming obese, because of laziness and are getting glued to technology. In the 1960s children used to be outside all the time but nowadays they are inside stuck to YouTube and rarely go outside.

Some experts argue that, life in the 1960s was safer for children. They cite that electronical devices are now a distraction from everyday life. In the 1960s kids were allowed to wander the streets knowing that they weren't in danger. Kids would stay outside and pass the time by playing games like; skipping, football and Hide-and-Seek. When she was younger, Mrs Johnson had fun riding her bike with friends. She would go out in the morning and not come back until the evening. At school, children felt less pressurised as there was no SATS (Standard Assesment Tests) to get worked-up about and no GCSEs (General Certificate of Secondary Education.) When she was at School, Mrs Johnson remembered doing country dancing as it was part of the Curriculum. No one can deny, people have more conversations face-to-face as people in 2017 usually have conversations on-line either by texting or Whatsapp.

On the other hand, 2017 has now been developed so that technology is a major aspect of everyone's life. Many people think that electronical devices are now a necessity to children's education; as interactive whiteboards and Ipads are a key to helping kids to learn. There is no doubt that children are allowed to go out alone but parents are now more knowledgeable about the dangers of being out with no adults (especially if they are out alone.) Kids now pass the time outside by; playing football, going for lunch, going round friend's houses or going to the park or skatepark. No one can deny, SATS help progress children in their learning - eventhough it can be a very stressful time - people also get a better understanding of what children know and don't know. Although meeting up to have a conversation can be nice; but is it always convenient? People in 2017 usually text or speak to people on the phone as they can do it anywhere.

In summary, many people assume that life in the 1900's was better than today', because they had more freedom. However, children still have freedom and are still allowed out but they just have to keep their parents aware of where they are. Kids can now phone or text their parents with the tap of a button - incase of any problems or emergencies.

Maisie Johnson

Was life better in the 1960s?

There is a lot of debate about, if 1960s was better than now. Many people think that 1960s was simpler: children were out more in the street or in their back-gardens. Others think that 2017 is great: children can contact their parents when in danger or make sure their friends are not busy. Schools in the 1960s disciplined children with stricter punishments but now kids are still disciplined but are the punishment strict now? Were they better in the 1960s?

On one side of the argument, some people believe that life was easier and simpler for children. Children in the 1960s enjoyed the company of people and seeing friends: there was no technology for kids to spend their life on. Kids leisure time was used by playing football, hopscotch, tag and lots of other games children made up. When he was younger, Mr. Standing remembered getting knocked out by a cricket ball. When he was 15, Mr. Standing liked to ride his bike down to the beach. He played a range of games like: football, tennis and Knock Down Ginger.
There is no doubt that, it was safer in the 1960s due to there being less cars on the roads which meant kids were safer playing in the streets. Parents weren't worried to let the kids go out as long as they came back at a certain time because there were less cars on the roads so it was easier to cross the roads. Kids were disciplined more with better punishments: the cane, standing in the corner and the slipper. These punishments disciplined and made the kids have more respect for people.

On the other side of the argument, some people think that now is better than the 1960s. People have technology now which is great in some ways; people can contact the police, their parents, they can talk to friends and play games on phones. Punishments today are less harmful to kids, teachers now put kids on a warning, then yellow and then red (when kids go on red they go to the head). Now there are better resources to teach kids like better technology for kids to interact with (Playing games about learning). No one can deny that, coloured TVs are more interesting than black and white TVs they had in the 1960s with only 1hr of kids TV. Now kids tv is on almost all day and adults have more channels so do kids. Those in favour of 2017 being better than 1960s would agree that there are more things kids can do. Skate parks are used a lot by kids because kids like doing cool tricks on them and some kids go kyaking on the river. There are many things kids do now that they would have done in the 1960s like: foot ball, criket and kids still play with dolls and plane models.

In conclusion, many people widely believe now is better due to the technology. Technology helps kids to tell people where they're going or just to contact people to go out. However, others believe that the 1960s was better due to kids having more freedom and having respect. Kids were out a lot more playing in the streets and had more respect for people around them especially adults.

Maisy Standing   Alexis Bell

Was life better in the 1960s?

There has been a lot of debate over whether these days or the 1960s were better. Nowadays children entertain themselves with technology. There is no doubt that technology makes life better and simpler. Instead of writing letters in hand and sending them through the post they can just use email and send it through the internet to someone's email address. If children -or adults- want to know something quickly they can just turn on their smartphone and type what they want to know into a search engine (GOOGLE) and get the answer in under 1 second; they couldn't do that in 1960. It's also much easier for teachers to teach as they can now teach from iPads and computers; whereas teachers back in the 1960s had to teach from notebooks. Now everything is coloured, instead of black and white, and schools all have HD 1080p smart boards. Many people think that life was better in the 1960s; not everyone agrees.

On the one hand, it is widely believed that life for children was easier in the 1960s. Without the distractions of computers children spent all day playing on the streets safer than our own. Children's leisure time was spent by playing games such as: golf, basketball and football which enabled children to socialise with their friends and have bags of fun. When he was younger, Mr Head liked to build go-karts and make tree houses. He also liked playing football with his friends and for Ware Youth FC. When he done his homework he liked listening to music – through his headphones – to help him concentrate. These days, children socialise between on-line societies where they've been struggling to make real life friends.

In the past, children had less pressure when doing exams (11+) because the teachers didn't give the children all the big build-up before. The teachers told the kids that they were doing a test and after, told them that they'd just done their 11 pluses. Whereas, nowadays teachers put more pressure on kids. Children now cripple under the pressure of big events. When he was a young boy, Mr Head used to get forced to eat school dinners that he didn't like and when he went swimming at school he said that the pool was as cold as ice; nowadays we have heaters in our pools at school. Children left school at 14 which meant they had a longer experience at work and were working by at least 16. It's right to say that nowadays, the days are getting warmer and kids are struggling to go outside and play with their friends without getting drenched with sweat; but back in the 1960s global warming wasn't such a big problem.

On the other hand, many people think that life for kids is now simpler. These days children can't go anywhere without using technology. There is more excitement in kid's now as they have video games to get over their boredom. Children can now still see each other's faces and speak to them through APPs such as: Face Time, Skype and WhatsApp. Children now have to stay in education until 18, which means they've had 4 more years of education and will have a better chance of getting a decent job and they will succeed more in life than 1960s kids. There are now more resources for education as teachers can now teach using technology and it really increases kid's knowledge and understanding.

In summary, although many people think that life in 1960 was better for children as they had less pressure and greater freedom. Children these days may have less freedom but they feel so much more cared for by their parents; they still do play-out but always keep their parents informed with information such as: when they're coming home, where they're going or if they've arrived somewhere. They do all this by the touch of a phone. Children today do cripple under SATs and GCSE pressure but have a good education non-the-less. They also benefit from uses of technology as they can speak to their friends even though they aren't near them. Children in the 60s did not have this luxury. There is no doubt that these days are better for children, don't you think?

Sam Head

Google

Was life better in the 1960s than now?

Nowadays, some people think that life today is better than the 1960s; children take electronics for granted and so do adults. In the 1960s children played on the streets and train-tracks and they could die and the parents would never know. In the 1960s children were fitter because they played more sports instead of playing on consoles or tablets. However kids can go to the skate park - whereas they didn't have them then.

On the one hand, it is widely believed that in the 1960s life was simpler than now for kids: it was safer back then because there weren't many cars and less pollution and there wasn't social media. It could be argued that children were more social then; they liked to play outside. Their leisure time was spent by playing more sports such as: football, rugby, tennis, riding bikes, swimming. Children would spend their time with their friends building dens, climbing trees. Some of our relatives were in the 1960s. When she was younger, Mrs Dunlop went to dance clubs, listen to records and went to the cinema to watch films. Also she got taught by really strict teachers; she wrote with fountain pens. When he was younger, Mr Samuel remembered being taught by nuns at St Cross school in Hoddesdon. The thing he did in his spare time was playing with toys and playing football in his back garden. Back then, staying inside wasn't really a must because children after school would go straight outside and go back in when they were hungry. In the 1960s, year 6 had to do a test called 11+, whereas now they are known as SATs. In the 11+ test there was less pressure put on children before the tests, but nowadays in SATs the teachers put alot of pressure on the children to do well.

On the one hand, many people think that life is better now because; the TV is coloured, there are skate parks, more channels on TV, social media, smart phones and other devices have been made. The school life now is a whole lot better because in the 1960s they had black boards but now we have interactive white boards and other devices. Such as computers and Ipads. There is no doubt nowadays sport is better because the clothing is better; e.g. in the 1960s the shorts were too short. The ground is more suitable for sports that play on grass e.g. football, tennis, rugby, cricket.

No one can deny, that life is better now because, the technology has improved by a milestone because if children are out they can phone their parents and they'll know where they are. The other reason is that the punishments have calmed down alot now because children used to get the cane but now they get the SHOUT!!

Jack Osford
Josh Samuel

Was life better in the 1960s than today?

There is no doubt, people enjoyed life in the 1960s, but it could be argued that nowadays is better even so. People cite that some changes from the 1960s have had a positive impact and some may be negative: such as children being hit by a cane when they're naughty, which is unacceptable now. No-one can deny, that there is more sports played now than in the 1960s for both genders (especially girls). Also, school was very different as they learnt without technology, as for now we have interactive whiteboards to help us learn.

Fashion in the 1960s was very wacky and colourful, but now there are a lot more casual looks! They used to wear patterned dresses and now more jumpers are worn.

Some experts argue that life for children in 1960s was simpler. Children could just walk into any street and play games, knowing there wouldn't be much chance of them being hit by a car (as they didn't have many cars back then.) Some people fear, that nowadays children are more pressured to do dangerous actions that friends may have told them to do, as for back in the 60s children lived an almost danger-free life with responsible actions. At school there was less exams or tests that needed to be done, they had the 11+ in primary school: this could possibly put less stress on the kids. Now in secondary school people have to do GCSEs, A-levels and mocks. Instead of GCSEs, they did O-levels when they were 16. The kids only really came home if they were hungry throughout the day, so they would just walk home and get some food (which the school did allow.)

However, many people think that life today is much better, for example: technology such as Ipods and computers which are improving educating young minds. Children can watch videos so they can learn visually as well as listening to teachers. Kids need the maximum knowledge as possible to educate their undeveloped minds, as they still have a lot of learning to do. Another subject that people strongly believe is that music now is better as they have a lot more of a variety of bands and solo singers. Kids also have mobile phones to contact home with, which is a lot more safer as children also have emergency numbers to call if they are in danger, hurt or in trouble; like the police, ambulance and fire brigade services. TV is one thing that has changed loads; now people have coloured screens and millions of channels! Back in the 60s they only really had three channels, one kids programme, and they had black and white screens. When she was a little girl, Mrs Upton enjoyed playing with her dolls and riding bikes with her brother. Many students at school have alot more choices for sports nowadays than back then. However girls can play more sport that boys would play, like football and hockey.

In summary, many people agree that the 1960s was better for children as they had more freedom but now kids are a lot more safer because they can have contact with their parents at any time due to the invention of mobile phones. Also, schools punishments are a lot more fairer as the children are not hit by canes or slippers anymore. Now they just get sent to the head office or put onto yellow or red. No-one can deny that children are better off in 2017!

Mia Upton

Was life better in the 1960s than today?

There is a lot of debate about wether the 1960s were better than nowadays. In the 60s children had more freedom. However the technology is better these days. Some people think that nowadays there is more pressure for children, but others disagree.

On the one hand, it is widely believed that life was more social and kids had more freedom in the 1960s. Children's health was checked regularly by the nurses including the nit nurse. The food in the 60s was delicous. When she was younger, Miss Whitfield had a hymn book to share with a partner and they sang together. She remembers the Friday best meal: Pizza, chips, Artic roll (a jam rolley polley with ice-cream in the middle). It could be argued that children were more social; they played lots of games outside such as: Ring-a-Ring-a-Roses, Basketball, Hop scotch, Football, dens and they went on their scooters and bikes. They also play board games such as: Kerplunk, Operation, Space Hopper Twister, Ji-Joe, Old Maid, Mouse trap, Ludo and played with toys such as: Rockem-Sockem Robots, Cindy doll, Troll dolls, action men, Dolls hous.

And Etcha Sketch. When she was younger, Mrs. Neighbour went outside and played games such as hopscotch and nought and crosses. Her favourite thing to do was to play on the tire swings with her brother and sister. Unfortunately today children are stuck in an internet world and are not sociable. In the 60s children were more appreciative of what they had e.g. they had less things and were harshley tought which made them be more appreciative of what they had (children are more spoilt now). Children were less epressured in their 1+ because they just thought they were doing a practise test. Also people in the 60s were unaware of Global Warming so no-one had to stress about it.

On the other hand, many people think that present day is better than the 60s. One of the reason's is that now we have more recourses for education such as: laptops, Ipads, interactive whiteboards and normal whiteboards. This helps because if a teacher needed to double check something they can look it up on the internet instead of flicking through a dictionary. Nowadays children aren't allowed to hit children and smoke in classrooms. No one can deny that if kids have a smart phone now it can't help them if they get kidnapped by a strange man/women they can call 999 to come and help them there is no doubt that public trasport (buses, trains and airoplanes) are faster and more comfortable to travel in now.

In summary, although there is a lot of debate that the 60s was simpler and gave kids more freedom, it is clearer that life is better now as it is safer because kids have smart phones to call emergency services. Children also play outside but not as much because parents look out for them more. Some fear that children get too pressured and don't work as well, but experts have seen that children are getting better grades since the education system changed. Children of the 1960s did not get as good education as ther were less recources.

Natasha Whitfield
Abigail Neighbour

Was Life Better In the 1960s Or Now?

There is lot of debate over whether life in the 1960s is better or not. Nowadays, people are using lots of different technology: from smart phones to game consoles. If children have smart phones it would help parents to know where their children are but it wasn't always like that. Back in the 1960s people had lots of freedom and could go anywhere. Now teachers had white boards and smart boards but in the 1960s they had chalk boards and taught from a text book.

On the one hand, children in the 1960s had lots of popular games such as: tag, football, hopscotch and skipping. Mrs. Fox liked to go out on her bike with her friends. Miss. Judkins liked to play board games with her dad. Mrs. Holman liked to play with her toy tree house and she also remembered there was no internet. It was widely believed that kids spent all of their time playing outside on the streets that were safer than ours. Nowadays children have more on-line friend than real friends, that wasn't the case in the 1960s. There was less pressure because there was less tests in the 1960s. If children had a test the teacher wouldn't tell you if it was a major test like the 11+. Then there was less pollution because of there being less cars and factories. Also people were fitter with less cars, so people had to walk everywhere and kids didn't have game consoles so played outside all the time.

In the 1960s girls and boys could only do certain sports, such football, cricket, basketball and many more. These days children have limited freedom so they can't go everywhere so it's safer. In the 1960s they went everywhere and more things happened. Nowadays there is lots of pollution because of the increasing amount of cars and factories people are less fit than in the 1960s because people played games more than going outside.

People think, that the 1960s were better with lots of freedom and less pressure when testing but other think it's better now because of technology in schools including tablets, computers and smart boards. Also more children have mobile phones so they can call their parents to let them know. There is no doubt that children are much better off now.

Jake Holman

Kieran Judkins

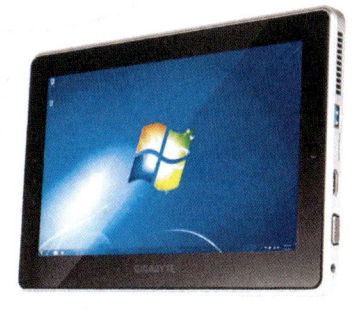

Was life better in the 1960s than today?

There is a lot of debate over life being better in the 1960s; however lots of changes have been made since then, many having a positive impact on today. When children arrive at school their teacher can almost immediately search up a fact or pull-up the classes task for that lesson on their interactive whiteboard instead of writing it out on a blackboard. Even the simple task of listening to music through a vinyl record, instead of quickly listening to it through a computer. Girls now can play every sport, whereas back then equality was not really a thing. Many people believe life was better in the 1960s; however many argue otherwise.

On one hand, it is thought that children had more freedom in the 1960s. Children then didn't have an electronic device to have their eyes glued to so they played outside. They played games such as: hopscotch; tag and other active and sociable games instead of playing on APPs on their phones and tablets. Mr. Freeman said that when he was a child he would ride his bike, climb trees, read a range of books and comics and walk his dog. He also liked to play a variety of sports; he would practice football in the street. People mainly liked to listen to rock music (which is very upbeat and lively) through a simple radio or vinyl record. Their parents allowed them to go meet their friends, walk to school, go for a bike ride and play in the street from a young age. Children met and played with their friends instead of texting them. There was little-to-no traffic so it was a lot safer to stand and play in the streets without their parents worrying about their safety.

On the other hand, it is widely believed that life is better now for children. Children now have electronic devices which are a great source of entertainment. Nowadays, children still play outside while also having the option to stay inside on their phones, computers and tablets that can also benefit the children's knowledge. People now can listen to music wherever they are with a tap on their phone. It could be argued, that parents now are over-protective, however many believe this benefits the kids and makes them feel cared for. Parents believe that if the child were to get hurt, they would know quickly or if there was an issue at school and they needed picking up early, they could come. Although some say otherwise many people believe technology benefits children. Schools point out that technology - such as interactive white boards have a strong, posititive impact on their learning. They further claim that it saves time as it is quick and easy to use.

In conclusion, although many people believe that life was better in the 1960s than today, as children had more freedom and they did not have technology crowding their lives. it is obvious life is better now. Children now do still play-out but (with the help of technology) children can call their parents using their phones wherever they are. No one can deny, technology is a great invention that has a strong positive impact on children's lives. The children of the 1960s did not have this splendid luxury.

Lydia Freeman

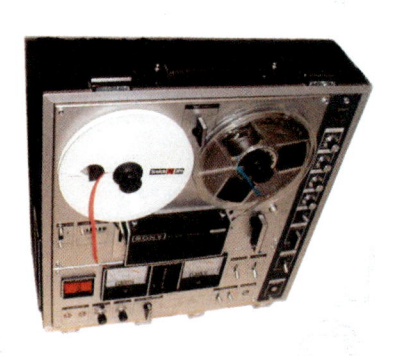

Was life in the 1960s better than today?

There is no doubt that life in the 1960's was good; but was it better than today? Many people argue that life is easier today but some think technology is taking over our lives. However, these days with one click of a button people can have: movies, music, information, social media and videos. In the 1960s, children had so much more freedom; but was that a good thing? Back then, children were allowed to go to here ever they wanted without their parents knowing; nowadays children have to stay in contact with their parents. Surely this was a safer way of doing things. Back then in school time they never had: Ipads, computers or smart-boards and the punishments were really bad because they would've got beaten with a cane, slipper or ruler by a teacher. Here are some points on the debate we have found.

On one hand, it is widely believed that it was safer in 1960s. Many people believe that pollution wasn't as high because there were less cars than nowadays which made the roads safer. Also children wouldn't have been bullied by other kids on-line as it didn't exist. It is argued that children were more sociable as they would have spent their spare time outside not stuck inside on the internet. In her spare time miss Shipton used to go to the park or play area. With her friends she used to go to youth clubs which included: dance, football, tennis and fishing. She futher cites that one of her worst memories as a kid was school, but more specificlay school dinners; she informs that she hated them and says that they were disgusting. Schools point out that in the 60s children were better behaved because of the stricter punishments and there was a lot less pressure: alot less stress. No one can deny that in the 1960s kids weren't judged on what they looked like but their personalities: sadly nowadays this has all changed.

On the other hand, many people believe that life is better now for children. One of the amazing things about schools today is that they are properly equipped with the correct tools to teach their pupils: Ipads, laptops and computers. Experts cite that the average living expectations has gone up since the 1960s because the advancements in technology has helped improve hospitals and their ability to save lives. Today many people believe that kids have it better off now, as kids have so much more choice: whether they want to play outside or stay inside but in the 1960s children were forced to go outside whatever the weather.

In summary many people believe that life in the 1950s was simpler, but is it better than today? Some may argue that nowadays kids have less freedom to play, but surely this is a better way of living!

Noah Milroy
Callum Smith

Was life better in the 1960s?

There is a lot of debate, about life in the 1960s being better than today; but is that the case? Back in the 1960s, schools were strict on discipline, for example: children got hit by a cane or a slipper but nowadays it is illegal to do that. Also, in the 1960s no one had a smart-phone, a laptop, an iPad or any other electrical devices. These days, everyone has a smart-phone which makes life easier for research, rather than going to a library. Also children love spending time on their consoles but back in the day, children didn't have them. Many people think that life was better in the 1960s; not everyone agrees.

On the one hand, it is widely believed that life was better in the 1960s. It could be argued that children had more freedom; children spent their time by playing football, rugby, tag and other activities there were. Adults trusted their children to be home on time. Children could play outside anywhere but if they weren't home on time they would get shouted at. When he was younger, Mr Springett liked to go to the cinema. Also he liked to cycle up the river, he played football and he played board games. At school in the 1960s there was a lot of hard work; children had to wear proper school uniform otherwise they would get the cane. Also, teachers taught on blackboards and they had to use chalk to write with. Nowadays children love spending time on their consoles and they do football, rugby, tennis, netball, badminton, table tennis, swimming and lots of other activities. In the 1960s it was safer for children because the streets were less busy. This was because most people couldn't afford a car so there were less cars on the road.

On the other hand; it is massively believed that life is better now. There are a lot more things to do nowadays including football, tennis, hockey, badminton, rugby and a lot more. In this generation, schools are a lot less strict because can wear the same uniform as the boys (girls can wear trousers.) Also punishment is less painful because now it is illegal for teachers to hit children in school. There is a lot more technology in schools. E.g. IPads, laptops and interactive whiteboards. Nowadays children play on their consoles and strengthen their online friendships and they can talk to each other using headphones. In this era, cars can travel much further and are more comfortable so people can enjoy a good car ride.

In summary, although many people think life in the 1960s was better for children with more freedom; it is obviously better now. Children today may have less freedom, but they have more technology (phones) so they can ring their parents if something is wrong or if there is an emergency. Children nowadays have a variety of activities to do such as organised football with coaches and a lot of other sports that are organised. The children of the 1960s didn't have this luxury.

Max Segust and Joe Robinson

Was Life Better In The 1960s Than Today?

There is a huge debate wether life was better in the 1960s or today. Childrens lives are now crammed with their online presence: from Ipads to smart phones they still feel the need to be present online. It wasn't like that in the 1960s though, because children were loads more social as their was no such thing as the internet. So children physically went to see their friends or family, ending up both being more social and healthy. because they walked to see them. A lot of people say that there was lots more freedom in the 1960s because people would just walk out of the house to go to their neighbour's house and just leave the door open and not have to worry about being robbed. Mainly because in each village, there was at least 7 police officers walking around. Mainly people think that life is better now but does everyone agree?

Many people believe that, in the 1960s life for children was very simple. When she was younger Mrs. Allan enjoyed making her own clothes whilst listening to music on her tape player e.g: Beatles, Rolling Stones and Mowtown. She also enjoyed sports like swimming, riding her bike, doing country dancing and playing netball. One of her favourite things to do was listen to music on her tape player and watch TV music shows e.g: Top Of The Pops, Pans People. Without being distracted by being present online, children spent all of their free time playing outside with their friends. They didn't have to worry about being kidnapped or runover becaus there was less cars and at least 7 police men in each village. The only time when most children would be inside was when children's TV was on (1 hour a day). Most people say that it is good that children could only watch TV for 1 hour a day, because now all children do is watch TV. Nowadays global warming is an awful, terrible issue in the UK but in the 1960s global warming was never an issue because there were hardly any cars therefore causing less global warming. School in the 1960s was better because there was less pressure on pupils because there was no SATS - which teachers now go on about from year 5 and pupils do them in year 6 - apart from the 11 plus test, which kids didn't even know that they were doing until the end. Also people could leave school at just 14 and go get a job, therefore everyone could earn more money at a young age.

On the other hand, now many people believe that school is better because kids are never hit by the cane and all of their toilets are inside. Teachers also have better teaching resources, such as the interactive whiteboard instead of chalk board. Also pupils now have a proper P.E kit but parents do have to pay for it. Pupils also get a proper P.E bag to keep their P.E kit in and P.E lessons are taught by the teacher, not using the radio. It is argued that in the 1960s girls had to make their own clothes, wereas now girls don't have to go through the struggle of making their own clothes and learning how to make their own clothes. No one can deny that in an emergancy people would call 999 right? But back then they didn't have phones so they couldn't call 999 so they had to run to a phone box. What if families didn't live near a phone box? Schools point out that if families were poor, then their child children would be forced to drink lukewarm milk (which is milk left out overnight).

In conclusion, although now there is more TV, many people question whether children need so much time watching TV. Back then children didn't have TV, so they were so much more social than now. They had much more freedom because children could just play out on the street and their parents wouldn't worry as long as they were back for dinner. Everyone has to agree that in the 1960s, without the stress of tests, life for children was so simple and fun.

Emma Gore and Sophie Duke

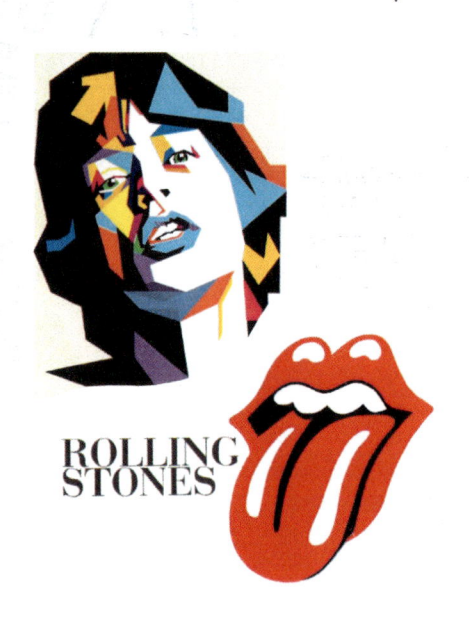

Was life better in the 1960s?

It could be argued that the 1960s were better than today with technology: from smart phones to laptops which is much easier for education, entertainment and at home. But it wasn't always like this. Back in the 1960s children weren't always entertained with electronics. They played with board games when they were inside and sports like football and basketball when they were outside. Nowadays children complain about detention but in the 1960s the punishments were much worse; like being hit by a cane or a ruler and having to stand in a corner (facing the wall) for the rest of the lesson.

On one hand, people think that life in the 1960s was much easier and better. Children's leisure time was spent by outdoor activities such as football, basketball and swimming for boys and netball, volleyball and tennis for girls. When he was younger Mr. Lakesic liked playing football, basketball and running around in the playground as well as riding his bike around the city by himself. In the 1960s, punishments were very educational because you wouldn't ever do it again. Kids either got hit by a cane, a ruler or they had to stand in a corner for the rest of the lesson. Music in the 1960s was interesting; people had to have very good voices and be good musicians because there was no auto-tune to enhance their voices. In the 1960s they had 11+ which was much easier because kids wouldn't even know that they did them, so it gave them a lot less pressure.

On other hand, others think that life is easier nowadays because of electronics. Technology is taking over children's lives. Children now play with: Xbox, ps4 and computers to pass the time. It's a great way to play because kids have a wide range of games to play with. Nowadays punishments are much more softer because the only punishment schools have is detention. These days, music is fast-beat and slow-beat. Children listen to pop music which is made by some artists like: Ed Sheeran, Chainsmokers and San Holo. In 2017, exams are very pressured on children because they have to study a lot for exams like: SATs, GCSE's and A levels.

In conclusion, many people believe that nowadays is more beneficial with technology because people can track other people by an APP on their phone. Kids still play outside, while having fun and if they're in danger they can call 999 and they will inform the child's parents so they know where you are. Therefore, there is no doubt that the 1960s weren't as good as now.

Dylan Lakesic + Jack Broughton

Was life better in the 1960s than today?

It could be argued, that life in the 1960s was better than today; is that really true? There is no doubt nowadays children have easier ways to learn: Ipods, Laptops. In the 60s they would have to go through a book but today children can just search their question in a search-engine. Children used to be way more free but was that a good thing? Although children aren't as free today; parents are protecting their children from harm. Cars have changed massively because they are now more comfortable and can travel much further. In addition, there are greater opportunities for all genders to take part in many sport and activities. Many people think that life was better in the 60s; not everyone agrees.

However, the 60s can be better in some different ways. It is widely believed that people were more free. Back in the 60s children had no technology so they went outside and played tag and hopscotch. When he was younger Mr. Kavanagh used to ride bikes and liked to build his own bikes. Where as today children are on their phones or Ipods 24/7. The curse of technology today is atrocious, for instance, terrorist attacks have been organised through Whatsapp groups, where as back then people could only contact by payphones or write a letter. Then there was less pressure at school for tests such as; the Eleven (nowadays the SATS). Many people think that schools put a lot of pressure on their students to do well in their SATS. The build up starts at Christmas and ends just before May. Children used to go out and play with friends whereever they wanted and they would be safe as there was a 1% chance of being run over as there was hardly any cars.

Less cars meant there wouldn't be as much pollution. Kids were told to be home by a certain time and if not they would have been hit, which punishes them and told them not to be late again.

On the other hand the modern day is also better than the 60s in some ways. Technology is key in peoples everyday lives. For instance many people think that if a child had a smartphone they could contact the police if a stranger was following them. Nowadays there are more resources for schools in education: Smartboards, Ipads, Laptops. No one can deny there is more of a variety of sports to pick from. There is also more equipment for sporting activities: better football goals, athletics equipment like safer javelins. Also everyone can travel to places quicker as most families have two cars.

Overall, even though people find the 60s better, alot more find the present day better for many reasons. First of all, there are better and stricter laws, but some could argue that children from a young age had more freedom. People today can argue that if their child was as free they could be in danger. Kids still play out, just not as much, as parents are just more protective.

Josh Kavanagh   Luke McCutcheon

Was life better in the 1960's?

Some people think that nowadays is better because of the mass of electronics. Many others think that the 1960's was better because it was more safer outside. Nowadays technology is better that the 1960's. It could be argued that nowadays music is more popular but the 1960's music was huge there were concerts every night! Supporters of the 1960's believed that then was the best time for going outside but some people disagree. School life in the 1960's was very disturbing: kids did PE in their underwear; had a nit nurse come regularly and were hit by a ruler on their knuckles; buttocks or their palm. In the 1960's food was quite similar to now: eggs; bacon or porridge but there was food like: Cocoa Flavoured Krispies and Crazy Cow.

On the one hand, it is widely believed that life outside was a lot safer outside in the 1960's because there wasn't many cars around. When she was younger Mrs Thorne liked to go swimming: played the guitar or she went roller skating (and broke her arm). She did a range of clubs: Brownies and Guides. Back then children were allowed to leave school at 14 years old. Every day kids were asked by their teacher if they wanted lunch at home. Parents didn't really care what their children did so they were allowed to go out in spare time to: the movies; played in fields; played board games; cycled or did their homework. Back then music was gigantic: there were concerts every night even though there were only vinyl records.

On the other hand many people think that life is better now. Children did PE in their underwear where now kids wear a PE kit. In those days they had one teacher but now children also have a TA. Back then kids had some electronics: now kids have: HDTV's; IPhone; IPad; Xbox; PC's and laptops. Schools point out that children were hit with canes but now they get sent to the Headmaster/mistress. A major cause of net getting into a grammar school, was that kids had to do an 11+ test but now children get in by putting in which school they want to go to. Now they have to do SATs to see what group they get put in.

I summary, although many people think that life now is better then. Children then had less technology, but they had freedom outside. Most people think that nowadays is better because kids have more things to do and they have more electronics: but back then the music was outstanding for the people in the audience.

Zachary Thorne and Luke Holman

Acknowledgements;

It is with great thanks and appreciation to all those who have helped either directly or indirectly in the publication of this commemorative book. All the children and staff of St Mary's have been highly supportive and thrown themselves fully into the events surrounding the school's 50th anniversary. Miss Alison George and Miss Kerry Charlwood whose initial thoughts and ideas inspired the idea for this book. Miss George further liaising with Rev' Ysmena Pentalow, our vicar at St Mary's Church, and with Rt Rev' Michael Beasley, the Bishop of Hertford who entertained and informed us all so well in a special assembly that he led. Further thanks to Mrs Joanna Bunce for playing so well the piano to accompany the children's rendition of 'All things bright and beautiful'.

Sincere thanks also go to Mr Kevin Speller, Mrs Jill Riley (formerly Homer), Mrs Melanie Piggott (formerly Ray), Mr Roy Hall and Mr Mark Berry some of the school's first pupils on the Kingshill site who visited us with such interest, humour and enthusiasm. Your knowledge and insights were invaluable; I hope we have captured some of them for future generations.

Special thanks to Mrs Margaret Meldrum, a former teacher, governor and special friend to the school over many decades, for sharing your insights and pictures that we have used in the 'Spot the difference' section of our book.

Mrs Barbara Sharman, one of the original teachers at the school in 1967, dropped in and shared a range of artefacts and information that were used on the hall display boards to help support the children's research. We particularly liked the photograph of the visit in the 1980s from Val Biro, the author of the 'Gumdrop' series of books. Barbara was also quick to praise the work and research of Mrs Jean Hobbs, the school's first deputy headteacher who sadly passed away in 2016. Thank you.

The works of the Rt Rev' Hugh Wilcock along with Jean Hobbs have been a huge inspiration and support in trying to pull together the very early history of the school prior to moving to its current location off Heath Drive. Particular thanks to Hugh's wife Barbara Wilcock for sharing our plans and well wishes with Hugh, and for sharing his photo that we have used within the book.

Behind the scenes there is the 'engine room', more commonly known as the school office; Mrs Judy Wareham, Mrs Joanne Scripps and Ms Tracey Powell. This book would not have happened without all the administration; typing, phone calls, e-mails, organising and refreshments. Particular thanks to Tracey for all the wonderful photographs that we have used throughout the book, helping to capture the magic of our celebrations. To Mr Graeme Wrenn, our site manager, for keeping us safe, clean and tidy, but most importantly big thanks for joining in and being part of the day; your hippy costume and dance moves was a true taster for the children of a bygone era! *(Please see the pictures below)*

Many thanks to 'Friends of St Mary's' and all the parents that gave their time, energy and money, particularly Lynne, Jenny, Sharon, Kerry and Emma for all their support in organising the 1960s/70s disco, raffle and Sports Day stalls that raised the money to fund this publication. Without you, purchasing this book for our families would not have been possible.

Most importantly indebted thanks to our teachers; Sarah, Clare, Fiona, Kerry, Peter, Tom, James, Joanna, Ali and Laura for all your planning, teaching, marking, feedback, creativity, patience, tolerance and perseverance in inspiring our children to write so well their articles included in this book. Also to our teaching assistants; Karen, Claire, Kathy, Kerry, Rebecca, David and Charlotte for most ably supporting and helping to guide our children into an unknown era, your engagement was inspiring. Thank you.

Finally, and by no means least to the most important people in any school; our children. Thank you for all your learning, creativity and considerable efforts in working together in planning, researching, drafting, reviewing, proof-reading and publishing all your articles that have been included in this book. Hopefully, one day in the future, may be in 50 years' time, you will once again look at this book and bring back some very fond memories.

Mr Andy Cosslett

(Headteacher 2005 to 2017)

Mr Wrenn demonstrating to Year 5 children the art of 1960's dancing!

Printed in Poland
by Amazon Fulfillment
Poland Sp. z o.o., Wrocław